BOOM TO BUST
The Great 1990s Slump

BOOM TO BUST
The Great 1990s Slump

John McQueen

The Bankruptcy Association
of Great Britain and Ireland

THIS BOOK IS A PUBLICATION OF

The Bankruptcy Association
of Great Britain and Ireland

4 Johnson Close
Abraham Heights
Lancaster
Lancashire
LA1 5EU
United Kingdom
Tel: (0524) 64305
Fax: (0524) 844001

ISBN 0 9518636 7 3

Made and printed in Great Britain by Biddles Limited, Guildford,
Surrey

Typesetting by Intype, London

Contents

Foreword

The story that unfolds in this book has been lingering in my mind, and in my heart, for quite some time, burning to escape. I have watched an economic disaster strike Britain, rip the guts out of the country and its people, with an ever increasing sense of dismay and anger.

I have tried to start this book several times over the past few months. I am an intuitive writer so I just know when there is something waiting to be written. Yet when I faced my word processor nothing happened. I simply could not find a starting point. I went through this frustrating performance several times, only to give up on each occasion.

Then, incredibly, like so many incredible things that have happened since I founded the Bankruptcy Association in 1983, this book picked the moment to write itself. I had been to London in June 1994 with Gill Hankey, who runs the Association with me. We had a series of meetings to attend which are described in the opening chapter. On returning from those meetings I wrote the regular quarterly newsletter for our members, explaining all that had happened. It was only after completing it that I realised the contents of the newsletter formed the perfect opening chapter for this book.

The newsletter was soon transformed into the first chapter –

Morning Trains to London – and the book was underway. The rest of the book then fell out onto the pages. It simply poured out. This story really must be told. It has a message for anyone who cares about our country.

That message is that we must start caring more about people than about money. We must care more about social conditions than the concerns of powerful vested interests who so dominate our lives. The capitalist system has its virtues, many of them. We must, however, as a society, recognise its many flaws.

Let this book now speak for itself. Let it tell its own story, the story of hundreds of thousands of people who have been the victims of the madness of the great 1990s slump.

John McQueen
Lancaster
Sunday 7 August 1994

PART ONE
Boom to Bust

1

Morning Trains to London

Gill Hankey and I caught morning trains to London on Friday 24 June 1994 abandoning the Bankruptcy Association to the capable arms of Gill's daughter, Joanne, who was to hold the fort for us. Gill and I had arranged to meet at one o'clock at Lloyd's of London. We had been invited there by Graeme King. He and his team are responsible for collecting in the losses of thousands of Lloyd's names. Lloyd's are the catastrophe reinsurers of the world. Now catastrophe had struck them.

Two hundred of their names are members of the Bankruptcy Association. They are faced with heavy cash calls as a result of massive claims against Lloyd's. These losses have occurred as a result of heavy environmental damage suffered in the United States and elsewhere.

My train pulled into Euston a few minutes before noon, about the same time as Gill's train was pulling into King's Cross. 'One Lime Street, Lloyd's of London,' I instructed the cabbie as I clambered into his taxi. As we ploughed through the traffic of central London it seemed bizarre that a few short hours earlier I had been in the relative calm of my bankruptcy bunker, as I call my office at my Lancaster home.

Twenty minutes later I was deposited outside that huge building, the home of Lloyd's of London. Gill, who had travelled from her

3

home in Hull, arrived a few minutes later. Between us, Gill and I run the Bankruptcy Association of Great Britain and Ireland which I founded in 1983 after my eldest brother, Jim went bankrupt. Gill has worked with me full-time since 1990 when the slump struck Britain. Between 1990 and the present day the Association has grown in size from a few hundred members to nearly three thousand.

We entered Lloyd's, dead on one as arranged, and were met by John Thompson, manager of the names support department, otherwise known as secretary of the hardship committee. John took us on a quick half hour regulatory tour of this amazing building which looked to me like a giant piece of plumbing. We were up and down lifts and escalators, whisked around the dealing floors, and we saw the famous Lutine Bell rung at times of bad news and good. On a podium facing the Lutine Bell is Lloyd's shipping register. This is a hand written record of ships lost at sea or grounded. Inspection revealed an entry showing that a ship had been lost that very morning as a result of a storm in a distant ocean.

There is also a little museum in memory of Lord Nelson. We looked at the log book written at the Battle of Trafalgar, open at the page where the famous signal 'England expects that every man will do his duty' is recorded. I was spellbound at the sight of that, as naval history had been a childhood fascination of mine.

After the tour we were taken to the office of Graeme King, senior manager of Lloyd's financial review department, otherwise known as their chief debt collector. We talked over a buffet lunch with a team of five people from Lloyd's responsible for collecting in cash from their names. A full and very frank discussion took place. It was also very pleasing to hear from Graeme King about the high regard he had for the Bankruptcy Association and its work. He had, he explained, been following and watching our work over many years.

The team of five appeared open and clear in what they told us. I was extremely impressed with their apparent honesty, although Gill had nagging doubts, which she vented on me later. The hardship terms being offered to Lloyd's names were spelt out to us. A matrimonial home of reasonable value could be kept until death. The hardship period would last for three years. During the period of hardship a generous proportion of income could be kept compared to that allowed in bankruptcy proceedings. After that period names would be able to keep all their income and inheritances.

I had already come to the view that the hardship terms were far more preferable than the bankruptcy option or an individual voluntary arrangement. Everything that we were told confirmed my views. It was clear in my mind now that most of our Lloyd's name members should take the hardship route.

There was talk, precipitated by Graeme King of Lloyd's, of the possibility of them making some cash help available to the Bankruptcy Association. I said that would only be acceptable if it could be used to benefit all the members of our Association, the vast majority of whom are bankrupt businessmen and women. They told us they were only prepared to help their own. I could not help making the comparison between the favourable treatment being offered to Lloyd's names, and the bulldozer of a legal machine that screwed the majority of our members into the ground.

We left that meeting at three and caught a taxi to our hotel. The heat was building up and we heard later it had reached one hundred degrees in London. It felt like it. After freshening up, we headed for the Insolvency Service headquarters in Bloomsbury Street. We had arranged a meeting with Michael Osborne, a Deputy Inspector General of the Insolvency Service. He is in charge of all the official receivers in England and Wales. We had forced this meeting at short notice and we had a blunt fifty minute discussion with him.

The background to this meeting was that three years previously we had adopted a policy of pressing every reasonable complaint we received from our members about their treatment by the Insolvency Service. As the complaints piled in, the Insolvency Service became acrimonious and we ended up with a great deal of bad feeling between us. We did this to wake them up to the existence of our Association. We not only woke them up, we also upset them severely. They have sulked ever since.

About a year earlier, Michael Osborne, then a newly appointed Deputy Inspector General of Bankruptcy, walked straight into one of the biggest rows we had ever had with the Insolvency Service.

He clearly did not know what hit him as we verbally machine gunned him into the ground.

Against this background I had telephoned Peter Joyce, Inspector General of Bankruptcy, some months previously and suggested a meeting. He said he did not think that would be helpful, given the unhappy climate currently existing between us. I left it at that, knowing we could force such a meeting if we so chose. That moment came after we were committed to the meetings in London with our members and with Lloyd's. I telephoned Peter Joyce on the Tuesday before our trip to London, but he was away until Friday. Gill then telephoned Michael Osborne requesting a meeting. He froze at the suggestion, but agreed to see us.

When we first arrived at the Insolvency Service there was an uneasy atmosphere. As soon as the meeting started Michael Osborne asked if he could speak to us off the record. We refused that request point blank, saying that all our business meetings were a matter of public record as far as we were concerned. I cannot guess what he might have said had we agreed to his request, but I doubt if he would have said anything of consequence.

I told Mr Osborne that we were angry and frustrated. We had been left to run what had now become an important public service, without any support or assistance from our own government, for 11 years. I considered it a complete disgrace the way we had been treated. If they tried to help us now, I said, we would refuse anything offered to us. He said he understood the sense of injustice we felt and that he sympathised with us.

He told us of his own grievances. He felt we were unfair. He investigated all our complaints, would discipline any member of staff who we could prove had treated a bankrupt badly, and he clearly felt we were hounding the Insolvency Service too heavily. There was an option being considered to privatise the Insolvency Service. With 1,000 jobs under threat, this had put a cloud over the entire department. In addition, like our Association, they had endured the horrors of this slump. We expressed our dismay that they might be privatised. We found them to be, like us, a generally benign and civilising influence in the bankruptcy world, although their incompetence annoyed us a great deal.

The bottom line was that we agreed that the pressures of the past few years had frayed nerves on both sides. We would start again with a clean sheet and see if we could work together without all the acrimony between us. We have been at this starting gate before. Both Gill and I, however, expect to be back at war with them soon because of the way they treat bankrupt people.

On leaving this meeting we bumped into Peter Joyce, Inspector General of Bankruptcy. He appeared from a lift with a fawning entourage of his staff members in tow. We have since wondered if this was carefully stage managed. He greeted both Gill and I by shaking our hands and asking after our health. We simply smiled acknowledgement – and then left.

Our main business meetings over for the day, we retreated to the pavement seats of a nearby pub in order to quench our thirsts in the hot afternoon. London seemed quiet, very quiet. I was looking for visible signs of economic recovery on the streets of the capital, but could see none. There were vagrants and the homeless wandering everywhere. We found this disgusting and embarrassing and I could not help but think of variants on Lord Nelson's famous phrase which we had seen at Lloyd's. Surely, I thought, England owes a duty to its people!

That evening Gill and I met Martin Levin, a London accountant, and one of the very first people to join our Association, to talk over internal association affairs. As the heat built up, a huge storm broke over the city and great forks of lightning struck the ground. It was dramatic enough to have photographs of it featured in The Times the following morning. We survived the storm and retired to our hotel for the night.

The following morning, Saturday, we strolled down to the Embankment and took a three hour boat trip up the Thames through London to the Thames Barrier and back. The Embankment was quiet, there were few tourists about and very few passengers on the boats out on the river.

In the afternoon we went window shopping in the Strand. It was quiet and there were half price sales on everywhere. There were also four shops offering bankrupt stock for sale with shirts on offer as low as £4 each. Even so, there were few customers. There were, however, a lot of glum looking shop owners and assistants.

Suddenly, and this could only happen in London, 40,000 Christians passed by us on a march for Jesus. They were hoping for the mass conversion of England. They failed in their attempt, and they made no noticeable impact on trade. We presumed they had no money.

Gill and I arrived at the Mermaid Theatre at six o'clock to organise the River Room there for the meeting of Bankruptcy Association members later in the evening. We were met with a friendly reception from the bar staff and conference manager. The friendly atmosphere deepened as members began to arrive just before seven. I was armed with £100 of Association funds and made a determined effort to buy every member at least one drink, and sometimes more. Nearly 40 members gathered in the space of half an hour. It was a very warm evening, although not as hot as the night before. We opened some large windows and a cool breeze from the River Thames opposite made it very pleasant.

I was very pleased to see two particular supporters, Ian Franses and his wife Vera. Ian, a London insolvency practitioner and also a publisher, had offered tremendous support and help for over ten years. He had always been there in background, amongst the woodwork, helping me along. It was highly appropriate that he should walk into chapter one of this book. Their daughter had graduated that day from Cambridge University, and they had hurried back to London from her graduation ceremony to attend our meeting. Ian's equally helpful partner, Eric Popat unfortunately could not join us, as he was celebrating his wedding anniversary.

About eight o'clock members gathered around Gill and I in a semi-circle as we prepared to address them. We had no plans or agenda and had intended just to speak informally. When I found myself staring into a sea of interested members faces I felt a little vulnerable. Gill sensed this and came to my rescue. She launched into a talk, telling the members the story of our Association over the past few years. I then took over, chatting for twenty minutes or so about our work and our thoughts for the future.

The members fired back, raising a barrage of questions and points about Association affairs. The discussions and questions were interesting and far ranging, along the lines of a good Question Time programme on TV or radio, but with our own special flavour. It was a very enthusiastic, lively meeting. Our members are bright, intelligent people. It became clear that some of them would like us to run the country.

On Sunday morning Gill and I again headed for the Embankment. We treated ourselves to glasses of orange juice on a restaurant ship positioned close to the House of Commons, and discussed all that had happened to us over the previous two days. We travelled back to Hull and Lancaster in the early afternoon, and we discovered later that we had both just sat on our respective trains for several hours, in pure thoughtfulness. There was much to think about.

2

Living Through the Slump

'It is good for us to encounter troubles and adversities from time to time, for trouble often compels a man to search his own heart. It reminds him he is an exile here, and that he can put his trust in nothing in this world.'
— *Thomas à Kempis (1380–1471)*

I am again in London. It is ten thirty on the morning of 20 November 1990. I am standing outside the headquarters of the Department of Trade and Industry with a group of Bankruptcy Association members waiting to see Minister of State, John Redwood. It is a historic day for the country. The vote is taking place amongst Conservative MPs for a new party leader which will result in the resignation, a week later, of Prime Minister, Margaret Thatcher. John Major will soon be elected to take her place and he will lead the Conservatives to another victory at the next General Election.

The Thatcher era has ended and a terrible economic slump for the country has begun. Interest rates have been high for so long in the battle against inflation that they have finally broken the backs of the people repaying mortgages and other borrowings. Property values in the South East have started to fall and this will

10

develop quickly into a nationwide collapse of the property market, with devastating consequences for millions of people.

Meanwhile, there are several other distractions for the country, aside from the resignation of Margaret Thatcher. Many people are outraged about the unfairness of the new community charge, commonly known as the poll tax, which has caused riots on the streets.

Abroad, Iraq has invaded Kuwait. The United States and Britain have begun pouring thousands of troops, tanks and planes into Saudi Arabia in preparation for the war that would soon follow. I am personally involved in this particular drama as my eldest son, John, a soldier in the Royal Artillery, is one of the first out there with his regiment. I am proud of his new role as a Desert Rat, but fearful for his life. He has been told that if Saddam Hussein attacks before the build up is completed, then his regiment could easily be wiped out. Thankfully, he survives the battles and returns home safely a few months later.

The streets around the DTI headquarters are thronged with TV crews and press reporters hunting for political figures willing to comment on the leadership battle. No-one takes any notice of our small group. Just before eleven when our meeting with the Minister is due to start, the Labour Party Chief Whip, Derek Foster, who organised the meeting, arrives in a taxi.

We are soon whisked up in a lift to the Minister's office, and a few minutes later are ushered in to meet him. Derek Foster explains to the Minister that the meeting is non political in nature, and that his own presence there is merely a courtesy. As later events proved, however, it became clear that the Minister took a very political view of the meeting.

Apart from Derek, in my party are Jane Lanham, a bankrupt divorcee who had been jailed; Tracey Lowe, the wife of a bankrupt, and Roy Whitman, an accountant who had gone bankrupt many years previously. Roy was also then an officer of the Bankruptcy Association. Across the table from us sit two stoney faced Insolvency Service officials, one of them being Desmond Flynn, a Deputy Inspector General of Bankruptcy, in charge of administration.

We state our points in a calm, articulate but determined manner. Jane complains of the harshness of her jail sentence. A middle-

11

class businesswoman with grown up children, Jane had gone bankrupt after her business failed. In desperation, she borrowed a few
thousand pounds from a bank without declaring her bankruptcy.
For this minor misdemeanour she went to jail for a year.

Tracey then explains she has five young children and will lose
her home because of her husband's bankruptcy. She asks John
Redwood to exclude the matrimonial home from bankruptcy. Roy
Whitman asks for a wide range of technical changes.

Finally it is my turn. I ask the Minister if I can read him a
prepared paper. I sense the tension mount in the Insolvency
Service officials opposite, and wonder what this means. I look
John Redwood directly in the face and read the following terse
statement:

*Thank you for agreeing to see us today Minister. I have waited
patiently for seven years to meet you, so I hope you will listen
carefully to a short written statement from me.*

*Our Association wants to see an end to the catalogue of pain
and suffering which we deal with daily. We want an end to the word
bankruptcy and to the present system of bankruptcy. We need a
new system of legislation introduced which treats people humanely,
protects their families and homes and which forces creditors to
come to arrangements with debtors. We see ourselves as fighting
against a social evil – the Insolvency Act 1986 – the most disgusting
piece of social legislation on the statute books of Britain today.*

*Bankruptcy could be ended immediately by modifying the present
voluntary arrangement and administration order procedures, and
by making such arrangements enforceable by the courts. It really
could be done at the stroke of a pen, Minister. I do not believe that
our current bankruptcy laws can be tolerated in a civilised society.
Over the last seven years I have spoken to many thousands of
bankrupts. They have all suffered cruelly under our bankruptcy
system.*

*An accountant wrote to me recently. He went bankrupt eight
years ago when his computer company failed. He had been earning
£50,000 a year as a chartered accountant and was struck off by his
institute. He told me he had gone through hell and that he wished
he had killed himself eight years ago. This was from a young man
of 35. It is just one example of the kind of letters we get. They come*

from accountants, doctors, solicitors, university graduates and the wide range of other professional and business people who make up the bankrupts of Britain. We get hundreds of letters like that one. This is what the bankruptcy system in the UK does to people and this is how it makes them feel. It treats people as if they are nothing, as though they do not exist.

The bankrupts of Britain are in agony, Minister. In agony. I know – because they have told me so – thousands of them. The law must be changed for the better.

I love my country and my family too much to stand aside whilst this carnage of bankruptcy takes place all around me. On current bankruptcy figures 360,000 of our fellow citizens will be bankrupted over the next 20 years. That is 360,000 families blighted by the obscenity of the label bankrupt. It is intolerable. It has got to be stopped.

In January this year BBC2 televised a documentary, IN FOR A PENNY, which highlighted the experiences of our members who were having their homes sold many years after their discharge from bankruptcy when they thought they were safe. Anything owned by a bankrupt before discharge from bankruptcy can be sold afterwards. The people involved, however, very often did not know that – nor did anyone in authority take the trouble to tell them or warn them. People in their seventies and eighties, some of them terminally ill, have had, and are still having, their homes sold many years after discharge. It is a national disgrace, Minister.

A few weeks ago I appeared with some of our members on the Kilroy TV programme. One of your parliamentary colleagues, Michael Grylls, was also on the programme. He said that people who fail in business ought to be given a medal, and he agreed that the law needed changing, having listened to our members experiences.

One of my sons is in the Gulf with the Desert Rats. If he is wounded or killed out there he will be treated with honour. Those who fail in business deserve respect and help too, not the undignified treatment they currently receive. How can you encourage entrepreneurs under such a system?

We now have nearly 800 members and the growth of our Association, along with our high media profile, has also provoked a crisis for us. We are now a large national organisation receiving thousands

13

of enquiries each year without any government support, and with only a very limited income. We are referred to on official government information given to bankrupts and are perceived by the national community generally as being a source of free and expert advice. In effect, we run an important public service, but without public funds.

We want three things from this meeting with you, Minister:

Firstly, your personal acknowledgement that our Association provides an important and much needed public service.

Secondly, your assurance that you will take our concerns for the need for changes in the law seriously. I suggest that some sort of working party should be set up, to include representatives of our Association, to look at these matters.

Third, and finally, I would like an assurance from you that you will look seriously at the possibility of providing us with some public funds to help us in our mainstream work, as well as providing financial support for a variety of research work which we believe needs undertaking in this field.

The formalities over, John Redwood shakes hands with us all and expresses his personal condolences to Jane and Tracey. He says we will hear from him shortly. We leave the meeting satisfied that we have presented our case well. I could not help but feel, however, that the Minister was something of a cold fish.

Weeks passed without a word from the Minister. The weeks turned to months. In January 1991 I rang Desmond Flynn at the Insolvency Service to ask what was going on. After investigation, it transpired that the civil servants in the Minister's office had lost all the paperwork relating to the meeting!

Shortly afterwards, a letter arrived from John Redwood rejecting all our requests and informing us that he intended to remove our name, address and telephone number from an official leaflet handed to all bankrupts. He put forward an absurd reason for this outrageous action, saying it would be helpful to us to remove our name from official literature because we were so busy! I was stunned. We had clearly come under political attack and we began now to feel the full weight of vicious bureaucratic power being arbitrarily applied against us.

A clear attempt to crush us out of existence was being made, although the Insolvency Service persistently denied this, and indeed, continue to deny it to this day. I have often wondered what lay behind that attempt to crush us. Maybe it was some petty, absurd motive. Or it may have been more sinister. Perhaps they were afraid that books like this one might be written one day to expose them. Several years on, I still neither know nor care, because they have failed in their purpose. Instead of being damaged by these political attacks, which have continued right up to the present day, we have grown from strength to strength.

I had to set aside all of the upset caused by these attacks on us, to deal with the urgent matter of increasing numbers of people joining the Association as the slump deepened into 1991. I was running the Bankruptcy Association single handed at this point except for some help from an unwieldy team of volunteers spread around the country. I was the one and only person actually answering the telephone, dealing with the correspondence, and, in fact, taking the full brunt of an increasingly busy Association. I was virtually at my wit's end. I needed help, but there was not sufficient income to pay for it, and the government had coldly turned down my request for some financial support.

Gill Hankey came to my rescue. Her husband's company had folded in 1990 and she had contacted the Association for help and joined as a member. I met her for the first time at a national meeting of the Association which we held at Reading University during September 1990, and there followed a lot of telephone contact over her case. Eventually, she volunteered to help with our work. She saved my sanity and the Bankruptcy Association.

We quickly developed a system whereby Gill took all the general inquiry calls on a telephone installed in her home on Humberside, whilst I just dealt with the advice line from my office, at my home in Lancaster. The system worked like a dream, and Gill and I have run the Association that way ever since.

It is important to explain here how Gill Hankey came to be involved in this critical period of the history of the Bankruptcy Association. There are many names on the Bankruptcy Association's roll of honour. Roy Whitman and Michael Sheldon-Allen are two of the most famous. The story of how they helped me in the early days of the Association is told in my book, *Bankruptcy – The Reality and the Law* which the Bankruptcy Association published early in 1992. Also mentioned in that book are Kay Short and Jim Freer who played a big part in those early years. For a short period two ladies from the South of England also played a role. These were Margaret Beaman and Terry Protheroe.

The heroine, however, of the last few years has been Gill Hankey. She, her husband, and co-director, Mike Byrne had formed a limited company, Astratech, in 1987 specialising in asbestos removal. When the company was formed National Westminster bank had offered them banking facilities. Another of the big four banks, however, courted them strongly for their business and the decision was taken to go with them.

The company quickly grew to a turnover of £1.1 million a year and gave employment to 44 men. By 1990, although trading conditions were not as good as in previous years, Astratech had a full order book and by their bank's own admission were solvent and profitable.

Then disaster struck. Their local bank manager rang to say he wanted to send in an investigating accountant. He assured Astratech that there was nothing to be concerned about. Within a couple of days an accountant sent by the bank arrived. He spent three and a half hours in the company's office and submitted a report to the bank that contained many inaccuracies. A few days later the same man returned introducing himself as an administrative receiver from the insolvency arm of the same company, appointed by the bank.

Four working days later the business was sold to a client of the administrative receiver for a knock down price. Although the directors of Astratech were instrumental in collecting in nearly all the money due for completed works, a sum far in excess of the overdraft, the administrative receiver's fees, taken out of the pot first, ensured that there was a shortfall of debt to the bank.

By then, some six weeks after the receivership, the new owners of Astratech had made huge profits, more than doubling the money they paid for the company. Contracts awarded to Astratech's original owners were completed, all of the company's assets were removed, and the operation was then closed down, leaving the directors and workforce unemployed.

The bank then asked for proposals from the directors to repay their shortfall, under the terms of their personal guarantees. The company having been destroyed, there was no offer the directors could make and the bank started possession proceedings against Gill's home. In an effort to stave off these proceedings, Gill and her husband immediately put their home on the market, asking £195,000, but there were no takers. In February 1992 a cash offer of £120,000 was received and instantly refused by the bank.

Eventually, the bank gained possession in October 1992. Gill, her husband and younger daughter moved into rented accommodation. At the eleventh hour a local authority bungalow was provided to accommodate Gill's elderly mother who had lived until then in a granny flat attached to Gill's home.

The bank then reduced the asking price for Gill's house steadily. As it was a large detached house in a rural area vandals soon move in and caused considerable damage. In April 1994, the bank handed over responsibility for the sale of the house, now virtually gutted, to the first charge holders on the property, another bank. No reasons were given. The asking price was reduced to £120,000, exactly the same price as the bank had refused two years earlier.

Due to the incompetence of the bank in failing to sell the house, and allowing it to be vandalised by taking possession, the position is fast approaching where Gill's husband, Ed might be bankrupted, and Gill could be in the same position because the house may now not raise enough to clear the joint first mortgage. Meantime, they are currently paying a rent on their new home which would have been enough to meet the mortgage repayments on their repossessed home.

Gill and her husband have lost their home, and face potential bankruptcy, because of their outrageous treatment by the bank who have bulldozed through their lives and their business without rhyme or reason. The bank has been utterly intransigent throughout, despite the fact that they have shot themselves in their own financial foot. This story is typical of the way the financial institutions have treated the British people throughout this slump.

At least something of use has come out of the tragedy that befell Gill Hankey and her family, in that Gill now plays such a major role in the running of the Bankruptcy Association. Our story, our fight for decent treatment for the bankrupts of Britain continues, sure footedly, day by day. We are firing back.

Throughout this slump, which I have already said began in

earnest around October 1990 with the collapse of the property market, I had generally been working seven days a week. I tried to steal the odd half-day or day off now and then but was usually punished for it if I did, with non stop calls from desperate people pouring in. Bank holidays did not exist for me. Gill endured similar hours on the inquiry line over in Hull. We worked at this pace, without a break, until April 1993.

During this period I was getting between thirty and forty calls a day from members facing or going through bankruptcy, and needing advice and help. One day during 1992, at the request of Tony Dawe, a journalist with The Times, I wrote an account of the calls I received one typical Monday. It was not published as promised, one of many broken media promises. It did, however, at least preserve a record of that day for posterity and gives the flavour of what I was dealing with daily throughout the slump. It ran as follows:

My first call is at nine in the morning when I open the advice line. It is from a man in Sussex running a chain of butchers shops going to the wall. The next call is from a construction company in Northampton. This business collapse is going to drag a father and his two sons into bankruptcy. The next call is from an East Sussex estate agent followed by an exhibition organiser from London.

By mid day half a dozen people have offered to shoot the Prime Minister. I always say there is no need as there are plenty of others willing to do that job when they get the opportunity. I usually try to make Monday a bad day for HMG and anyone connected with them. If I am going to fax out any inflammatory press releases or rude messages to Insolvency Service officials, it is invariably on a Monday.

All afternoon the calls flood in. A retired army major in Wales is going bust because his egg business has failed after a partner cheated him. A debt collector from Southampton is next. No one has any money to pay their debts! A TV presenter from a regional TV station follows on. She and her husband are going bankrupt because his TV company has failed and they have negative equity in their home. Then a stained glass window manufacturer from Essex calls. The churches have no money to spend either. Nobody

18

has any money it seems. Surely, I ask myself, someone must have money. Where did it all go?

In between calls I keep in close touch with Gill Hankey who runs the general inquiry line over in Hull. We keep each other sane by swapping crazy stories and making black jokes about the country, the government and Peter Joyce's brother. Peter Joyce is the Inspector General of Bankruptcy and therefore our official arch enemy. As one incredible story of disaster follows on from another, we always convince ourselves that the last call was a hoax call from Peter Joyce's brother.

Peter Joyce must have a lot of brothers though, as the next call is from a holiday complex, a former Butlin's holiday camp, going broke. This is followed by a Somerset farmer and then an estate agent from Wiltshire.

On and on it goes. Gill gets light relief by dealing with endless calls asking about bankruptcy sales. These calls are nearly always from Bradford. We are convinced that everyone in Bradford is now dealing in bankrupt stock. We, however, do not.

My main entertainment is usually provided by press enquiries, most of them daft. The Kilroy TV programme seem to ring us every week. Will we provide them with twelve teenage children of bankrupts to talk about the problems of being the teenage children of bankrupts? Will we provide them with twelve couples who have stayed together through bankruptcy? Will we provide them with twelve couples whose marriages split up because of bankruptcy? No, no, no is the reply every time. Our members are real people, not animals in a zoo. But the Kilroy programme never gives up. I expect next week they will ring up asking for twelve one-legged bankrupts to talk about the problems of being bankrupt with one leg.

I stop taking calls at about five in the afternoon, grab a bite to eat, and then exchange a series of faxes and telephone calls with Gill, as we catch up on each other's day and the administrative tasks we share.

At seven in the evening the advice line opens again. The first call is from a headmaster in Cheshire going bust. He was caught with two properties and a bridging loan after a promotion led him to move, just before the property market collapsed. Next is a marketing consultant from Burnley, then a doctor from Yorkshire bankrupted

by a builder after he extended his surgery and the Family Prac-
titioner's Committee failed to pay a grant. Then an airline pilot
going broke because he borrowed money to learn to fly. Next an
Italian restaurant owner rings from Essex followed by a husband
and wife and son and daughter partnership, all going bankrupt
through running a pub.

Exhausted, I take the final call of the day about nine in the
evening. It is from a lady of 60. Her advertising business has failed
after thirty years trading and a quality Sunday newspaper has sent
in heavies to seize her business equipment. The bailiffs threatened
to rape her and her young assistant, she tells me. She is alone in a
large house in Birmingham and she has a loaded revolver in her
lap which she has bought that day. She tells me she is going to blow
away to hell the next bailiff to walk through her door.

I ring Gill just after nine to check that we are both still sane. We
both express our daily disbelief at what is happening to this once
great country of ours. I then have a shower and retire to my local
pub to rest my brain over a couple of pints. I ponder over the lady
with the revolver and wonder if she will shoot herself or the bailiff
tomorrow. I never find out.

This description of one day during the slump gives a brief
glimpse of the madness that Gill and I lived through. It became
clear during 1991 that an entire generation of entrepreneurs were
dead or dying. I am one of the few people in Britain who really
understands what this means, talking as I did with thousands of
bankrupt people throughout this nightmare.

When the slump first struck in the autumn of 1990 businesspeo-
ple began to call us from the South East. Their banks were pulling
the rug from under their businesses. They had overdrafts secured
on houses which were beginning to accrue 'negative equity'
because of collapsing property values.

Every kind of business suffered. People were ringing us who
had been running successful companies for upwards of thirty years.
Then the building industry collapsed – it seemed in its entirety.
We were swamped for a year with calls from property developers,
builders, architects and others in the building industry, all going
to the wall. I think nearly every property developer in the country
must have gone out of business. If there are any left they should

be given a gold watch, a knighthood and a free passport. There is a deep silence from that industry now.

The slump hit the South West in the summer of 1991, like a hurricane let loose from the South East. Pubs and hotels began to go down in droves as the tourists dried up. Towns like Bournemouth and Weymouth were devastated.

In June 1992 we held an Association meeting in the Prime Minister's constituency of Huntingdon, the birthplace of Oliver Cromwell, at The George Hotel. Virtually every one of a dozen shops between that hotel and the Prime Minister's favourite restaurant had closed down. It seemed a twee market town in conservative heartlands, but every shop was offering stock at reduced prices and there were sad signs of the slump everywhere.

I had written to John Major inviting him to attend this meeting. Hardly surprisingly, he declined the invitation, although his private secretary rang to apologise for this. An angry meeting of our members took place. One of them, Michael Flanagan, a bookseller facing bankruptcy, had stood against the Prime Minister in the recently held General Election, as an independent candidate. On the election platform with John Major on the night of his victory, the bookseller had placed a copy of my recently written book on bankruptcy in the Prime Minister's hand, and elicited his promise to read it. Another member, a former Conservative councillor from Huntingdon, was in a fury about the banks and the Tory Party. They were all crooks and gangsters to him. Thatcher's 1980s 'yuppies' were also at this meeting in force, except now they were bankrupt and destitute. I was staring into the face of Margaret Thatcher's legacy to Britain.

Shortly after this meeting the media seemed to wake up to the fact that something was going sadly wrong in the country. On 7 August 1992 I was interviewed by BBC1 TV national news and a bulletin went out on the one o'clock, six o'clock and nine o'clock news programmes with me complaining that many bankrupt people were suffering and that some were reduced to living in garden sheds. As a result of those broadcasts, the Daily Mail rang me that same day and asked me to dictate an article over the telephone to one of their reporters. I spent two hours dictating this piece, but again it was never used, although I was assured it would appear the very next day.

We, as an independent Association, were battling against a huge government propaganda machine which was pouring out ludicrous comments about 'green shoots of recovery' and other such nonsense. This has continued ever since. The government has spent the last few years convincing themselves that there is no slump and trying to convince the British people of the same lie. They are still doing it, even as I write.

By 1992, however, the evidence of the slump was everywhere. Travelling about the country to various Association meetings there was nothing but depressing conversations to be overheard from people on the streets, in trains and on buses. The slump worsened throughout 1992. Scotland and the North of England now began to feel the hammer blow of the downturn. The entire business community of Britain was in a kind of agony.

The peak of the slump was reached in the first quarter of 1993. More than 10,000 people went personally bankrupt in those three months. This total beat the number of bankruptcies during the whole of 1989. The whole country seemed depressed. The slump could be physically seen. Every town and city I visited had sales in all the shops. There was a noticeable lack of traffic and shoppers. In the United States, one publication started a new cartoon feature. It was based on a ragged Brit, in a low paid job, trying to eke out a living in miserable Britain, full of unhappy people.

It was hard to believe I was living in the country that had defeated Hitler. The morale of the whole population seemed to wither and finally collapse. A World in Action TV crew came to see us whilst making a programme which was transmitted on 28 September 1992. They were amazed to discover the scale of the misery, and it turned out that many of their friends and relatives were teetering on bankruptcy. Subsequently, TV people of all kinds went bust as that industry was itself devastated.

By early November 1992 the position in the country was so bad that Gill Hankey was broadcasting on the BBC World Service about the state of the nation, whilst I was broadcasting on BBC Radio 4 on the same subject. It was as if the whole world was going broke. It seemed that almost every day Gill or I, or others who were helping us then, were appearing on TV or radio programmes, commenting on the slump in the country. There were also many articles about the work of the Association in national

newspapers. Sometimes several national newspapers carried articles about us, all on the same day. We lived through many hectic,
action packed days, our lives completely taken over by our work.
It was a time of total mayhem, for us, and for the country.

About this time, to add to the craziness, I was invited to be a
Citizen Ambassador to China, with all expenses paid, representing
an institute founded by former US President, Dwight D. Eisen-
hower. This institute runs the Citizen Ambassador Program
intended to foster links between the peoples of the world. I was
asked to lead a team of American bankruptcy experts to advise the
Chinese government on a bankruptcy system for their Southern
Provinces. I was proud to receive this invitation. It was trans-
atlantic recognition for the Bankruptcy Association's achieve-
ments, although this did not make up for being ignored by the
British government. Sadly, due to the circumstances surrounding
me, I could not accept the invitation. I had too much to do in
Britain.

Then tragedy struck. Whilst living through this mad, sad period
of our social history I received the devastating news that my
younger brother, William, had contracted cancer. He was living in
Ireland, having married an Irish girl, and they had two young
children. I went over to Ireland and saw him for a few minutes,
just hours before he died. He died in Dublin City on Sunday 22
November 1992 aged just 39. His death left a large hole in my life
– and a larger one in my heart. Even now, nearly two years on, I
am still struggling to come to terms with his death.

I was stunned by this terrible loss. I could not take it in properly,
surrounded as I was by the madness in the country. I could barely
believe what was happening to me and to people all over Britain.
Each and every day seemed like a nightmare as I struggled with
my grief and a never ending stream of calls.

Christmas 1992 arrived and that was a nightmare. Calls to the
Association faded out as they always do over the Christmas period,
and grief for my brother flooded in. Being so busy, I had not had
the time to grieve properly. Nor did we have the usual, family
party on New Year's Eve at my home, a traditional event. We
were too shattered as a family.

Our telephones began ringing again as soon as the new year
opened. I did not know it then, but we were entering the peak of

the bankruptcy storm. Articles on the Association continued to appear in the national press throughout 1993 including large pieces in The Times, Observer and the Daily Express, amongst others. We continued to feel that the whole country was going broke. It was now clear that a wholesale slaughter of the business community was taking place.

I kept going at this exhausting pace until April 1993 when Jim Freer, then an officer of the Bankruptcy Association, took over the daytime advice line for four months in order to give me a break. This left me with only the evening shift. As the pressure came off, I immediately fell ill and went down with bronchitis. This completely flattened me, physically, for a fortnight. Looking back over those months and years, I sometimes wonder how I bore the pressure for so long. I could not imagine re-living such an experience, and I hope I never have to again.

I am, however, also glad I did do it. I have that proud feeling of 'I was there on the big day – doing my bit.' Gill and I lived every waking minute of this terrible slump in a unique and special way. We were there at the coal face every day supporting the victims. We witnessed a huge social drama unfold on an unprecedented scale. We saw, at first hand, a piece of our country's social history being made. It is important to record it here, because there will be those, including just about everybody in the media and the political establishment, who will try to cover it up. They will attempt to bury this bit of the past, if they possibly can.

From April 1993 to the end of July 1993 I rested and recovered properly from my illness. I was also able to go through a proper grieving period for my brother. Gill was reporting to me daily that the pressure of calls had fallen off. It felt like a period of calm after a great storm. The second quarter's bankruptcy figures for 1993 at last showed a fall, down 20 per cent on the first quarter.

There were, however, still a lot of bankruptcies on a historical comparison and they remain high to this day, with over 14,000 bankruptcies recorded in the first six months of 1994, the latest figures available. It looks as if there will be a high number of personal bankruptcies until the end of the century. We are still a very busy Association.

I want to explain now my repetitive use of the word slump, as opposed to the word recession which has been more commonly used by politicians to describe the economic events of the past few years. My edition of the Oxford English Dictionary defines recession as meaning a temporary decline in economic activity or prosperity. There are no signs yet that the problems currently being experienced are temporary. The same dictionary defines the word slump as meaning a severe fall in prices and a sharp decline in trade or business. With the collapse of property values, and cut price sales in just about every shop in Britain, there can be no doubt that we have suffered from a slump, a severe one, not merely a recession. Furthermore, as I write this in August 1994, there are few signs of recovery – although you would not think so, listening to the BBC.

As August 1993 approached. I felt refreshed and renewed. I planned to take over the advice line completely again, and to rationalise the running of the Association as our shoe string budget could not cover the costs of maintaining the team of officers we then had. I took the hatchet out and sadly cut the team right back to just Gill and I running the Association full-time. It was a hard, but necessary decision, and proved to be the correct one. We struggled to survive financially even after these cut-backs. Our Association has always lived hand to mouth, like most of our members.

Since that time, Gill and I have worked hard at building up the image of the Association as a user friendly organisation. We have developed a wide range of 'hands on' services for our members. The Association has changed beyond recognition over the past few years, primarily because Gill and I make such a good team, although we both work from our own homes more than 100 miles apart! We have many more back up services for our members, as well as regular newsletters and meetings. Four years ago we were little more than an emergency telephone advice service. These days we physically handle individual cases for our members and deal with all kinds of complex problems and negotiations. If, four years ago, we offered a Ford Escort of a service, the comparison would be that we now provide a Rolls Royce of a service.

We have also developed a wide range of personal contacts within the financial and legal worlds. We have specialists who help us in a wide range of matters. In particular, a firm of insolvency lawyers, Carrick Read Insolvency, with offices in Leeds, Hull and

London, have been especially helpful in dealing with a number of difficult cases and tricky points of law.

In June 1994, Andrew Laycock, a lawyer from that insolvency firm, drove over from his Leeds office to see me. He came for a general chat about various legal issues which were concerning me, and to discuss a bankruptcy textbook I wanted him to rewrite. I had spoken with Andrew many times on the telephone over the past five years and I was very pleased to finally meet up with him.

We took advantage of the sunny weather and sat outside in my garden. Before starting a long discussion on a wide range of matters I played him a recording of a BBC Radio 4 'In Business' programme which had been broadcast on Sunday 29 May 1994. This strongly featured the work of our Association. Peter Day was the presenter, he had interviewed me at length and had expressed his admiration for the work that Gill and I were doing.

Peter and his producer, Colin Wilde had then gone over to interview Gill in Hull. Gill had arranged for Chris Garwood, another partner of Carrick Read Insolvency, to be at her home and take part in the programme. Chris, a specialist bankruptcy lawyer like Andrew, has also supported and helped us with our work.

Andrew Laycock and I listened to the recorded programme on which opinions were aired by myself, Gill, Chris Garwood and other well known characters from the world of bankruptcy. Two of our members, Chris and Julie Percival also took part, going bankrupt live on radio! They were an impressive couple and made some impressive comments on their bankruptcy experiences.

I was pleased to hear at the end of the programme Steve Hill of Coopers & Lybrand, a long time arch opponent of mine, calling for an earlier discharge for the majority of bankrupts, reversing his previously reported views. The programme made me feel that other people were coming round to share my own long held opinions.

Shortly after meeting Andrew Laycock, Gill and I boarded our trains to London for the meetings which I described in the opening chapter. I had many thoughts passing through my mind as I made that journey. I thought back to the first ever meeting I had with the Insolvency Service. That had taken place one freezing cold January day early in 1984. I had felt very much alone then, indeed at one point I had been dubbed in the press as 'a lone crusader.' Two junior civil servants at the Insolvency Service tried to rubbish me, claiming that bankrupts deserved all they got, saying they were either crooked or incompetent.

I knew that was not true. My brother Jim, whose bankruptcy prompted the creation of the Bankruptcy Association, was a fine and honourable man, and a good businessman. Events, as they often do in business, had conspired against him to bring about his downfall. I was determined to fight back against whatever was thrown at me.

Now, ten years on, I was travelling to London under very different circumstances. I had built up an Association of several thousand fine, bankrupt people and achieved widespread support for our work from a range of people and institutions. It was a very different John McQueen who went to London ten years later. People were now not only willing to listen to me but were actively seeking my views. Even the high and mighty at Lloyd's of London wanted to meet me.

There has never been any glory in my work for the Bankruptcy Association. I have spent too many years being rubbished and sniped at for anything I ever do in the future to go to my head. Gill Hankey can vouch for that, and for the scale of the rubbishing attempts.

What I do feel now, however, is a tremendous satisfaction in being able to speak out on behalf of a downtrodden, broken section of our national community. I get a lot of kudos from that. I have always liked a good fight with those in authority who, invariably, are incompetent, if not plain bent. The bankruptcy world fits that pattern exactly.

As I approached Euston and made ready to leave the train, my thoughts slipped back to an emergency meeting of Bankruptcy Association officers held on the Isle of Arran in 1990 when we discussed the future of the Association. The slump was underway and I was beginning to crumple under the strain of it, although Gill soon came to my rescue. After the meeting we went to the home of one of our members, Norman McIver.

Norman was about to be bankrupted after 20 years building up a business on the Isle of Arran. He had lost everything and was about to have his beautiful home repossessed. Both he and his

27

wife were terribly distressed. We sat chatting and having a few beers, whilst tears were shed all round. Norman was planning to return to his native New Zealand with his wife to seek the support of his family, leaving grown up children in Britain.

After a while, I went outside and sat in his front garden. It was a beautiful summer evening and the sight that greeted me was stunning. In front of his home lay Holy Island, recently purchased by Buddhists to be used as a religious retreat. It was a magnificent sight.

Norman came out after a while and sat beside me, handing me another can of beer.

'It's not a place you want to leave, John, is it?' he said.

As I looked across at Holy Island, I felt that I could have stayed rooted where I was for ever. Yet, even where I was, on the Isle of Arran, which seemed like the most beautiful place on God's good planet, I was sitting alongside a man whose life had been shattered, and whose family would soon be separated because of the slump and our wretched bankruptcy laws.

I looked beyond Holy Island, across to mainland Britain, and knew that over there many thousands of other fine individuals like Norman and his family were also being put through the same torture.

'No, Norman,' I agreed. 'It's not a place you want to leave.'

I looked at Norman's face, weary with the suffering and stress he had been through, and then across again at the beauty of Holy Island.

And I knew then, I just knew, that the work of the Bankruptcy Association would go on, and that one day we would succeed in our crusade to change the law.

3

Unaccountable Accountants

I understand the title of this chapter is the same as that of a book being written by Professor Prem Sikka, and Member of Parliament, Austin Mitchell. These two people are part of a small, but growing, number of professional people and politicians who are beginning to share the long-standing concerns of the Bankruptcy Association. They, like ourselves, are particularly concerned about the lack of regulation and behaviour of insolvency practitioners.

The bankruptcy world, from the point of view of those who administer the system, is very small and incestuous. There are three components to it.

There is the Insolvency Service. This is a government funded Executive Agency staffed by a few thousand civil servants. The Insolvency Service oversees a chain of official receivers offices around the country. Their job is to investigate the reasons and causes of personal bankruptcies and company liquidations. The Insolvency Service also police both bankrupts and the bankruptcy system, in general.

The second component is the judges, registrars and lawyers who specialise in bankruptcy matters. These would be numbered in hundreds, rather than thousands.

The third component is made up of around 2,000 authorised

insolvency practitioners, organised into several hundred private firms. They specialise in acting as trustees in bankruptcy and liquidators of private companies and they have supporting staff numbering a few tens of thousands.

Compared to most other professional groups, this is a tiny world. All the key players are personally known to each other. Until quite recently the simple existence of this specialised world was probably unknown to the vast majority of the general public. As a result of the slump, this is no longer true.

More than 100,000 people have suffered the humiliation of having their personal lives and financial affairs examined in detail at official receivers offices throughout the country. Thousands of people have been arraigned before judges to have their homes torn from them. Hundreds more have been severely punished for trivial bankruptcy offences. All of these people have seen the bankruptcy machine at close quarters. Many despise it as much as the writer.

It is this third component in the bankruptcy world which has drawn the most media attention and general opprobrium to itself – the insolvency practitioners. Cases such as the spectacular collapse of the Maxwell empire have brought them to the attention of both politicians and the public alike. The equally spectacular fees that many of the larger firms of insolvency practitioners have charged, to dismember such businesses, has caused some alarm.

The accusations of chicanery, fee-rigging and downright dishonesty amongst this group of people have been fairly constant. However, they have survived all these attacks on them, even if they do show signs of being somewhat winded by all the criticism. It is hard to imagine any other professional group surviving such a battering without some government intervention to make changes.

How have they managed to do this? The main reason is that their victims cannot bite back, and because no-one else really cares. It is also because of a long tradition and prejudice, enshrined in our insolvency laws, that implies that a bankrupt person or company deserves no rights, no respect. They are dead things, to be despatched with what is, in effect, a legal hatchet.

A bankrupt person or company has few rights. A common criminal can commit heinous murder, rape or arson and the state will provide him with a criminal barrister and all the resources needed to defend such charges. Yet a bankrupt person or company can be financially dismembered and wrecked without the opportunity to mount a realistic defence.

The law, in effect, says that a trustee in bankruptcy or a liquidator can do no wrong. The courts traditionally, and currently, have a prejudice against the bankrupt person or company. This prejudice is endemic and needs to be experienced, to be fully understood.

The reader will be in no doubt by now of the writer's strong feelings on this subject. I am totally against the present bankruptcy machine in general terms. I am, however, aware that there are many fine people working both as insolvency practitioners and for the Insolvency Service whom I admire and respect, and indeed, a small number of judges. However, there are equal numbers of sleazy, bent, devious characters too. Such is life. In the bankruptcy world, because of the way the laws are angled, the damage that the bad guys can do to bankrupt people and companies far outweighs the good that the good guys can do for them. It is the system that stinks.

Strong words like these require strong evidence. I have masses of it. When I founded the Bankruptcy Association more than eleven years ago, one of the first people to contact me was a former employee of the audit section of the Insolvency Service. In breach of what was then the Official Secret's Act, he sent me files on hundreds of liquidation cases he was involved with. He also provided me with copious notes of complaints he had made to his superiors, requesting investigations into various matters. His reward was to be transferred, against his wishes, from the Insolvency Service to the Shipping Service of the DTI. Nobody can cover things up better than the Civil Service – they are age old masters of the craft.

Also, on my desk as I write, is a book entitled Indictment. The author, David Morrell, was the chairman of Mitchell Construction, a company which he had built up over many years until it achieved an international reputation so great that it was awarded the contract to build part of the famous Kariba Dam in Africa. The company was put into receivership and later into liquidation under the most alarming of circumstances. Mr Morrell outlines in

31

detail the chicanery that was employed against the company by many of those involved in its receivership and liquidation.

The receivership and liquidation of Mitchell Construction occupied several years during the mid 1970s. Since then David Morrell, who is now in his eighties, has been fighting in the courts and through his books and articles to get many wrongs righted. He has fought determinedly, backed by his shareholders, for more than 20 years. He fights on now, to use his expression, to the death. Such is the sense of anger and injustice he feels about the treatment of his company by the receivers and liquidators.

My original intention at this point was to introduce and reproduce the full script of a programme broadcast by BBC Radio 4's File on 4 programme of 21 June 1994. The programme examined several case studies of companies which had been ripped off by their liquidators. The BBC initially gave verbal permission for this, but I felt we ought to have written authority, as I had no wish to infringe copyright. The protracted discussions which followed proved ludicrous. I could write a book, indeed have done, in the time it takes some petty BBC bureaucrat to make a decision on such a simple matter.

In any event, on reflection, I felt such an account might bore the reader. I think it sufficient to briefly describe the content of the programme. Any reader, with the patience to deal with BBC bureaucracy, can obtain the transcript and/or a recording from them. To sum it up, the programme examined several case studies of companies that had been wound up. They found that assets of these companies had been sold off at ridiculous knock down prices. In one case, the liquidator himself had bought the company that he was liquidating. This is both illegal and in breach of all known professional ethics.

One director of a company complained that the investigating accountant brought in to investigate his company was totally incompetent and inexperienced. The director only managed to save his firm from disaster because his best friend was a very experienced London barrister. The others were not so lucky. Details of a catalogue of abuse by liquidators against companies then followed.

At the end of this programme the point was made that the

accountants responsible for disposing of liquidated companies are, simply unaccountable.

4

The Big Boys go Bust

The years 1989 to 1994, the five year period which this book largely covers, were years in which many famous household firms went to the wall. They were years that saw Robert Maxwell die at sea under mysterious circumstances and his huge empire collapse, with the Mirror group pension scandal ensuing leading to Maxwell's two sons being charged with various offences.

They were years that also saw Lord Beaverbrook go broke and Asil Nadir go into bankruptcy, after the collapse of the Polly Peck companies. George Walker, another high profile figure, also went bankrupt and there were other notables and companies that went to the wall in quick succession. Even the pop star, Bob Geldoff, went bankrupt for a short time, under ludicrous circumstances. A bankruptcy order was made against him in London whilst he was on tour in Japan. Apparently he had failed to pay a car hire bill to a German company. The bankruptcy was quickly annulled and the bill settled, but it shows just how easy it is to bankrupt someone in Britain.

Bankruptcies of the famous drew huge media coverage and speculation, demonstrating yet again how the British love to denigrate successful people, when their luck runs out. This is a great British disease, and whilst the British have many fine qualities, this aspect of our national character dismays me.

In particular, I was outraged at the spectacular rubbishing that Robert Maxwell and his sons had to take. The fact that Robert Maxwell was a greedy and arrogant man was apparent to all whilst he lived, although few dared say so then. After his death those closest to him, many of whom were on huge salaries, were the first to pillory him.

I was one of the few people who gave press and radio interviews defending Maxwell. I saw him like many other desperate business-men who make last ditch, dangerous moves, in an attempt to save their businesses. In Maxwell's case, the consequences were much more far reaching in the damage done to others. However, the scale of the damage in no way heightens the scale of Maxwell's motives. You could just say he was unlucky. And – who knows – if he had lived he might well have pulled through his troubles. It is easy to knock a man, but how many people have built companies the size of Maxwell's in one lifetime, starting from scratch, without a bean in their pocket? That was some achievement, whatever the end game result.

As the publicity surrounding these famous bankruptcies esca-lated I received a letter from one William Stern, who, in an earlier decade, had been the biggest bankrupt in the world. He wrote to me complaining that everytime someone famous was made bank-rupt his name and photograph featured in the press, along with that of the recent bankrupt. He said there was no escape from the past for him and his family. Criminals had better protection than former bankrupts, he argued. He also sent a cheque for £100 to help with our fight on behalf of bankrupt people.

Over the past few years, because of the losses of the Lloyds of London insurance market, many well known people have joined our association. There are lords and knights of the realm, retired generals and admirals and a wide range of highly respected people in our society. All are now facing possible ruin because of their losses with Lloyd's.

The Lloyd's fiasco is instructive in many ways. It shows that people, no matter how many there are, or whatever their influence on society, cannot stand against institutional money machines. Lloyd's is preparing to gobble up many of its names lives, as I write. The Times reported in its issue of 6 August 1994 that Lloyd's had appointed a top firm of London lawyers to take proceedings against those names who had not applied for hardship terms, and who were refusing to pay their losses.

A whole layer of top people in the country will be devastated by this affair. The same issue of The Times reported the story of a retired solicitor and Lloyd's name who had suffered tens of thousands of pounds in losses. His wife was quoted as saying that they may well lose their home. They were devastated.

On the day I wrote this chapter I received two letters from Lloyd's names. One was from an agent of Lloyd's who had not only suffered losses himself, but was being sued by other names who felt that they had been 'set up' by him. He pointed out that nearly all agents were names themselves and in the same boat.

The other letter, an even sadder case, was from a young man who had been employed by an agent of Lloyd's. A condition of his employment was that he would also become a name. He had no capital, so his employer arranged a bank guarantee of £25,000 and said he would cover any losses, if they occurred. When they did occur, his employer went bust, Lloyd's drew down on the bank guarantee, and the young man now faces bankruptcy. All he had wanted was a job. The pressure has caused him to split up from his wife and two young children. They are in a terrible state.

This is happening to thousands of real people who are Lloyd's names. Some will manage a reasonable future on hardship terms, but others face bankruptcy and destitution. The money machine cannot be stopped from its purpose whatever the cost in human lives and suffering.

It should be clear from these stories that the bankruptcy machine is a very powerful wrecking device. For a debt as small as £750, anyone, however mighty, can have their lives shredded by this monstrous machine.

I had cause to ring Graeme King, the chief debt collector at Lloyds, on the morning of 11 August 1994. Letters and telephone calls from our Lloyd's name members had cast doubt on his statements made at our London meeting. In particular, he had strongly implied that the names who had settled their losses had done so willingly. I had since learned that bank guarantees had simply been called in by Lloyd's. They had really plucked the money from their names' pockets. Graeme King immediately conceded this point. I told him we had been frank with them in

London and we had expected the same treatment, in return. Gill Hankey's doubts had proved correct. I now think that there may well be a can of worms waiting to be opened at Lloyd's, and that the story is far from over.

'Is Lloyd's going bust?' I asked Graeme King. 'No chance,' he replied. 'We have £15 billion in the bank.'

'I cannot cope with these telephone number figures,' I said. The scale of the Lloyd's operation is beyond ordinary human imagination. As Graeme King put it to me 'Lloyd's is more like a government than an ordinary company.'

He also conceded during our conversation that UK bankruptcy law was too strict on people, and that bankrupt people should be allowed to keep a home of reasonable value. He was, like many others before him, now agreeing with my way of thinking.

As I put the telephone down, I thought that Graeme King sounded much more tense than on previous occasions. Perhaps his job was beginning to get to him, and I was glad I was not in his shoes, high up in that strange Lloyd's building. The conversation with Graeme gave me much to think about, as did the whole Lloyd's connection. Sources inside the Corporation of Lloyd's had variously described their names as fortune hunters or gamblers implying they deserved all that was coming to them. I could not envisage the highly respectable, intelligent, prominent Lloyd's name members of our Association falling into either of those categories. I thought of them much more as lambs, who had been skilfully fleeced. The fact that Lloyd's were helping them beyond the strict letter of the law, implied that they felt that way too.

After speaking to Graeme King I received a call from the son of a 76 year old bankrupt man. He said his father's trustee was going to force the sale of his parents' home. His mother was 70 and had lived in the house for 30 years. If she lost her home, he told me, it would kill her.

That call brought me down to earth with a crash. This is how ordinary folk are being treated. This was the bankruptcy machine in action as usual, crushing the wounded. This was the machine that we were out to fight. These were the ordinary people that Gill and I helped each day. These were the people who really mattered.

I also thought back over all the sneering, jeering comments

made against us and our members over the years. I thought of the invective rubbishing the Association had endured from the Insolvency Service, and from the Lord Chancellor's Department, who had joined with them in that process. I thought of the 300 copies of my last book which I had sent to Labour MPs before the 1992 General Election. They had been completely ignored by all but one of them, Austin Mitchell. I thought of the hundreds of letters sent to politicians of all colours, including all top ministers. I thought of my own MP, Elaine Kellett-Bowman, who has studiously ignored me for more than a decade. We are fighting the entire political establishment, who seem bent solely on their own self aggrandisement, giving little thought to the real issues which dominate peoples' lives. I also thought of the glib comments from bankruptcy judges. One had recently told a Bankruptcy Association member: 'The bankruptcy laws are too soft. In Victorian days I could have sent you to jail.'

These are the sneering people who run the system. These are the people who ruin the lives of thousands through their lack of care, their lack of morality and, primarily, their lack of humanity. This is what the Bankruptcy Association fights against.

5

The Middle Classes go Bankrupt

The world is money driven. The money beast, as D H Lawrence described it, is the beast on which all men feed, like lice. They will do anything for it, sell their bodies, and even their souls, in their desperation to get their hands on the filthy lucre. Such is life. In the hard battle for survival, men and women battle to get their hands on money. We are not far advanced from the primitive societies whose survival depended on the results of the daily hunting expedition. In many ways we are a more cruel society. Primitive societies shared their food, the equivalent of their money income. We do not. We wrestle with each other daily trying to get a bigger share for ourselves.

This slump has effected the whole country, but it is the professional, or middle class, strata that has taken the severest hammering. I have described in the previous chapter the problems facing thousands of Lloyd's names but one hundred thousand other people have gone bankrupt too, in the past three years.

I was in the middle of writing this book when I received a call from a couple in Carlisle. They had been running a hotel in Scotland and were in a very distressed state. They said they needed to see me urgently. I agreed to their request and they rapidly drove down to Lancaster.

They competed with each other in their haste to blurt out their story. There was immense strain showing on both their faces and I could feel the pressure they were under. In fact, I could almost reach out and touch it.

It transpired that the husband, after a successful sales career with a large company, had gone into business for the first time in Devon, during 1982. He bought a small hotel and built up the business. In 1988, at the height of the property boom, he received an offer he could not refuse and sold his hotel for £250,000, taking a huge profit.

They then settled into a period of retirement, although the husband was still in his early 50s and his wife in her late 40s. Soon the husband decided to go back into business. They spent two years tracking down a hotel they liked. They made thorough checks and they even stayed in the hotel a few times as guests, to ensure that all was as claimed.

In 1992 they talked to their local bank manager who said it was a good idea and that the recession was over. It was agreed that they would put down a deposit of £150,000 on the purchase price of £350,000 and that the bank would advance the rest as a loan, leaving them with £100,000 working capital.

Within three months of taking over the hotel it became apparent that the whole thing was a pig in a poke. The books had been cooked. The room rates they were told were being charged were wildly inaccurate, as were the food prices. In addition the recession was not only not over, it had only just begun to strike hard in that area. The husband then had a nervous breakdown and his wife had a minor stroke.

It was a complete nightmare and they poured more and more money in, until there was no more. The bank suggested they put a management company in to run the hotel. It turned out they were not a management company but simply asset strippers. After trading through the best months of the year they made the couple an offer of £120,000 for the hotel leaving them penniless and with a shortfall to the bank.

They could not believe what had happened to them. They were two very experienced business people who had previously run their own successful hotel. They had thoroughly researched their new venture, and took all the advice they could from professionals, such as their bank and their accountant. Yet they were effectively wiped out within months. Their lifetime of effort in accruing £250,000 was all to no avail. They had made one mistake, and one only. They also had no effective legal recourse against anyone.

Such tales of disaster and chicanery are now common currency within the British business community. All vestiges of business morality have simply disappeared.

There is also little morality amongst the professionals who are supposed to be there to help and advise when their clients face problems. In general, the majority of accountants and solicitors are unwilling to continue their support of clients when they realise there may not be money available to cover their fees. By washing their hands of people in this way they may protect their fee income, but they have brought themselves into disrepute at the same time. It should also be said here that few accountants and solicitors have been schooled in bankruptcy law and their advice is often misplaced, if not completely incorrect. Approaching such a professional can often, therefore, leave a debtor in a worse position than ever.

A top headmaster in the country is a member of the Bankruptcy Association. He is not a bankrupt. He earns £45,000 a year. He is probably the envy of many people, including most of his large staff. He was, however, caught in the web of the slump. On being promoted to his current position he had to move several hundred miles. He put his home up for sale, a smart detached house in the South of England. He obtained a bridging loan to buy a new property for himself in the North of England, a standard transaction, and a safe one throughout the past century. He bought his new house as the housing market peaked and then collapsed.

He could not sell his former home except at a huge loss, leaving him with a shortfall to the building society. His new home also dropped in value dramatically. The upshot is that he is currently in a voluntary arrangement paying £1000 each month to his creditors. He no longer owns his own home, but rents a house for £600 a month. His wife is on the verge of a nervous breakdown because of all the trauma. He is at his wit's end trying to support his daughter through university, helping his wife to cope, running one of the biggest schools in the country and trying to come to terms with what had happened to himself and his family, as a result of his promotion.

Another member of the Bankruptcy Association is a young dentist who came top in his dental course at university. He set up his own practice with a £100,000 bank loan aiming for the highest standards and ideals. Two years later, he is bankrupt with his life in ruins. He could not make his practice pay. High standards and making a living in dentistry just do not go together, he told me.

He will never practice dentistry again, he says. He has borrowed £1000 from a relative and has rented a house in Florida. He intends to fly out there shortly with his wife and three young children, never to return. The bravery of this young man amazed me. He had trained for a professional career, tried it for two years, been ruined for good measure, and now he was chancing life in a new country, far from home. Such is the state of Britain today.

These are just a few examples of the many thousands of professional people who have contacted the Bankruptcy Association over the past few years. They come from every walk of life. All have similar tales to tell. Many of them have had their professional status stripped from them when they have gone into bankruptcy. This action has deprived them of the opportunity to earn a living and to practise their profession. It should be remembered that the taxpayers of Britain have paid tens of thousands of pounds to train them for their jobs. The position of these people is, quite frankly, ludicrous. The bankruptcy system is barbaric. It needs overturning in its entirety, tomorrow, before it completely wrecks our country.

6

Boom to Bust

I am not an economist. Nor would I pretend to be one. I think I would be fair in describing myself as an intelligent, middle aged man with a wide experience of life. I also have two university arts degrees and a teaching certificate to my name. I hope I could also be described as having a good common sense grasp of the national affairs going on around me.

More than most people, I was asking myself what on earth was happening to this country as the slump struck, deepened, and then ran on. Like everyone else, I have been utterly confused by the plethora of economic analysis in the media, and from government, as to why things are the way they are.

I think it was Margaret Thatcher, who first blamed this country's ills on a 'world recession.' I am not sure how the world can go into recession, or if the term has any real meaning. Even in the middle of a slump in Britain there are boom areas and industries, and the majority of the population are at work. To talk of the world being 'in recession' is, to my mind, nonsensical. The world economy surely is what it is, an ever surging tidal sea running up one shore as it pulls away from another.

It is true, as John Galbraith points out in his brilliant book, The Culture of Contentment, that the world capitalist system is very sick. He points out that the economy of the United States went into severe recession in the second half of 1990 and that the effects of this spread to her trading partners in Canada, Europe and beyond. However, this would only have a minor effect on the world as a whole. Britain did not just go into recession, like the United States. It nose dived into a severe slump.

As well as listening to the ridiculous statements generated by the government, and circulated by the media, I have also been bombarded with many other economic theories. These have been sent to me by a wide range of characters, not only from all over the country, but from around the world.

Many are very interesting. One in particular, which I received from an engineer in Scotland, argued that the cost of all goods purchased in the British Economy exceeds the amount of wages paid out. Thus, his argument runs, for consumers to buy all the goods being sold, either private or public debt must increase. He enclosed statistics which appeared to support the truth of his arguments. This sort of treatise may or may not be true, and I am not sure where these kind of economic theories lead us. I have a file full of various economic notions, some fanciful, some attractive, but all leading nowhere, it would appear.

For these reasons I was strongly attracted to one, and one only, of the various missives on the economy sent to me during this slump. It was from an Eric Wye of Guildford, Surrey, a civil engineer who had followed economic events in Britain from 1974 onwards, with some trepidation. Eric Wye was Deputy Borough Engineer for Guildford when he retired. He had spent 39 years working for local authorities. He sent me his own analysis of what had caused the slump, and it had the smack of plain common sense truth. It also matched the thoughts tumbling around in my own head. His analysis of what went wrong in the country makes, to my mind, compelling reading and runs as follows:

WHY THE BUBBLE BURST

1974: The long awaited local authority reorganisation was effected by amalgamating small authorities into units about the size of County Boroughs. The office of Borough Engineer and Surveyor in the 'real' local authorities ceased to exist, after developing and evolving over a period of 100 years, with tremendous loss of expertise and experience. Senior staff in the new Boroughs created mini empires for themselves, taking over various functions, including – importantly – planning functions. The local expertise on planning matters was lost, a crucial mistake. The average cost of building land, with planning permission, was £50,000 per acre.

1975: Inflation, which started to rise after decimalisation four years earlier, was now rampant under a Labour administration. There was hesitancy in the housing market and land prices were static.

1978: Inflation continued to rise and the 'value of the pound in your pocket' deteriorated. Local planners stuck to the County Council post-war policy of no development in green belt areas. Major house builders only managed to keep operating by winning appeals against refusals for building development. The average cost of building land rose to £80,000 per acre.

1980: Now under a new Conservative administration, the Thatcher government policy was home ownership for all. Planners continued to refuse development in green belt areas. The average cost of building land rose to £100,000 per acre.

1981: The opportunity given to tenants to purchase their council houses had become an attractive proposition. Planners continued to resist any building in the green belt. The average price of building land rose to £200,000 per acre.

1982: The increases in the cost of building land had pushed up the cost of new houses so much that existing houses were becoming more attractive and their values were rising. Planners continued to resist all development in the green belt and the average price of building land, with planning approval only being won on costly appeals, rose to £300,000 per acre.

1983: The economy was growing. The value of houses built just after the war under licence for under £3,000 were now fetching up to £50,000. The 'two up, two down' town centre cottages, sold for around £1,000 between 1946–1950 were now changing hands for £30,000. The average price of building land rose to £400,000 per acre.

1984–1987: The housing bonanza continued with planners still refusing to grant planning permission in green belt areas. By the end of 1987 houses built in the 1960s for £10,000 were now fetching £130,000. The average price of building land rose to a staggering £800,000 per acre.

1988–1989: These are the crucial years. The economy was booming. Builders continued to sell houses even though the average cost of building land was now £900,000 per acre. Over the last few years existing house values had risen so much that second mortgages were readily available for new cars, home improvements, holidays abroad, etc. People were still buying new houses in a variety of sizes and at a wide range of prices. Self-employed building trades-men were earning £400 to £500 a week and their labourers about £300.

The Chancellor, Nigel Lawson, in his Spring budget of 1988, announced one mortgage relief per property instead of one per person, from 1 August 1988. Predictably, there was a mad rush to get on the housing 'band-wagon.' The huge demand sent house prices soaring, especially on smaller and older houses, and 'gazumping' was rife. Any saving made by having more than one mortgage relief was quickly swallowed up in increased prices.

The sudden surge in borrowing prompted the Prime Minister to declare that this was 'inflation – which costs jobs' and base borrowing rates started rising. These rose from 7.5 per cent in June 1988 to exactly double that by October 1989. Mortgage interest rates rose by a similar percentage in the same period. This increase in interest rates signalled the end of house buying and an end to the prosperity of the 1980s. The housing bubble burst open in the year to October 1989 and collapsed in on itself like a punctured balloon.

1989 TO PRESENT: House prices tumbled and the property market virtually collapsed. Estate agents, large and small, go bust in droves. In some towns in the South East every estate agent went out of business. Properties worth £250,000 at the height of the boom struggled to find buyers at £80,000. Millions found themselves caught in 'negative equity,' a hitherto unheard of term. People found themselves trapped in homes with mortgages much higher than the market value of their properties.

I think the above analysis is as good an account of the cause of the slump as any to be found. This account of what happened matches exactly how we at the Bankruptcy Association saw it. The property developers and builders went down first as the housing market collapsed like a punctured balloon, especially in the South East of England.

An economic atom bomb exploded. Imaginary money, i.e. constantly rising property values which had been propping up business expansion and a consumer boom, was no more. The booming 1980s were shown to be what they really were, an illusion and a confidence trick, perpetrated on the people by the financial institutions and those in power. Everyone had fallen for it.

As the dust began to settle on the collapse of the housing market, complete panic struck the major banks as their balance sheets began to show huge losses. They began pulling overdraft rugs from under the feet of businesses at the first sign of trouble, cutting off cash flow to the business community at a stroke. The domino effect set in as businesses collapsed, dragging each other down. Entire arcades of shops began to go bust, as consumer credit dried up and sales fell off.

In acts of unparalleled self mutilation, the government with its policies, the financial institutions by their panic actions, and the planners in their stupidity, decimated the British economy. The incompetence of those who run the country is breathtaking. It proves beyond a shadow of doubt, the ability of the British people to absorb anything thrown at them by those who rule over national affairs.

People in Britain are now paying the price for the incompetence of their rulers. In a bid to cut the public deficit created by the slump, the unemployed have come under attack, as have absent fathers, those on invalidity benefit, and other vulnerable groups who have come into the sights of the government. The government needs someone to kick, to blame for our troubles. Those in government should, instead, take a cool look at each other, and blame themselves.

7

The Statistics

I was attracted to the title of a book analysing the failings of capitalism, especially British capitalism, by Charles Handy, a famous analyst, management theorist and former chairman of the Council of the Royal Society of Arts. Handy's book, The Empty Raincoat, refers to an open air sculpture in Minneapolis. Handy regards it as a symbol of what is wrong with British capitalism. People are not destined to be empty raincoats, he claims. They are not numbers on a payroll, role occupants or statistics in some government report.

I know just what Charles Handy means. I feel the same way. Each human being is a unique miracle, a part of the vast miracle of life and human history. To some people, especially governments, these unique individuals are just numbers, just statistics to play games with. Let me take a look at the numbers.

Statistics can be confusing, misleading, and sometimes just plain wrong. Bankruptcy statistics sometimes suffer from one, or all, of these common flaws. Different kinds of insolvency are sometimes lumped with bankruptcy numbers. Company failures and personal bankruptcies are sometimes added together to give a total of business failures. Some statistics try to separate consumer bankruptcies from business bankruptcies. It causes constant confusion to people in the media trying to paint a picture. I am reminded too of the famous saying: 'There are lies, damned lies, and statistics.'

Some basic statistics available, however, show the dramatic increase in total bankruptcies over the past 20 years. These illustrate the huge surge that has occurred during the slump. Readers may find slightly different figures elsewhere for the reasons I have outlined above, but the figures which follow, provided by the Insolvency Service, give a good indication of the true number of individual personal bankruptcies over the past 20 years. It should be pointed out that even the figures given here are slightly inaccurate. The number of bankruptcies up until 1989 are inflated by a few percentage points because they include some other types of insolvencies which are not true bankruptcies. From 1989 onwards they are accurate.

PERSONAL BANKRUPTCIES 1973–1993

1973: 3,363
1974: 5,191
1975: 6,676
1976: 6,681
1977: 4,078
1978: 3,526
1979: 3,500
1980: 4,038
1981: 5,151
1982: 5,700
1983: 7,032
1984: 8,229
1985: 6,778
1986: 7,155
1987: 7,427
1988: 8,507
1989: 9,365
1990: 12,058
1991: 22,632
1992: 32,106
1993: 31,016

During the first six months of 1994 there were 14,003 bankruptcies. This is a provisional figure, provided by the Insolvency Service, and may be subject to slight adjustment later.

Slight recessionary periods in the mid 1970s and the early 1980s can be easily identified from these figures, as can the huge snowball of bankruptcies that began to build up from 1990 onward, reaching its peak during 1992/93.

Readers need to be aware that it has been variously estimated that for every personal bankruptcy there are between 5 and 10 other business failures where businesses close, but do not go bust. For every business that is closed by a bankruptcy order, many escape this final humiliation, usually by the skins of their teeth. People close their businesses, having lost their homes and all their investments, in covering their debts.

The true damage caused to the British business community by this slump cannot be calculated with any accuracy. The figures show, however, a startling rise in personal bankruptcies from 1990 onwards. They continue to run at unprecedented levels. Beyond doubt, the figures tell us that an entire generation of entrepreneurs have been, and are being, incinerated.

PART TWO
Across the Borders

8

Scotland the Brave

Scotland is my ancestral and emotional home. My father was Scottish, and although I am English born, I always feel more at home in Scotland. It is where my soul dwells. When I cross the border into Scotland, my spirit always lifts. Scotland has played a huge role in the story of the Bankruptcy Association. Without my strong family links with Scotland, I doubt very much if the Bankruptcy Association would ever have been founded.

The links run deep. My paternal grandfather had the same name as my eldest brother Jim, the brother whose experiences led me to found the Association. As a child I heard little mention of this grandfather. My father rarely spoke of him. All I knew was that he had been a labourer before the first world war. He had married my grandmother in 1902 at the age of 24 and my father was born four years later, in 1906. During the first world war my grandfather had served in the Black Watch and fought at the terrible battle of the Somme, in which he was wounded.

Returning home to Scotland, he could not settle down to married life and soon afterwards abandoned his family. He then took to a solitary life on the road becoming known as 'The Rovin Boy'. During the 1930s he was once featured on the front page of the Daily Express. He had walked the length of Scotland and back one hundred times.

When I was a young man, a Scottish labourer employed by my brother Jim, told me that he remembered my grandfather from his own boyhood in Glasgow. Each year my grandfather would work his way through that great city, sharpening knifes and saws, to earn a few shillings. He was famous to all the boys in Glasgow. I also learned that he had died in a tent, near Dumfries, aged 71, during the extremely cold winter of 1947. I presumed he had died of pneumonia.

My father visited him as he was dying. He had not seen him for nearly thirty years. My mother, who was pregnant with me at the time, accompanied him. She said their reunion was one of the most moving events she had ever witnessed. That was really all I knew about my grandfather during my childhood. There were few photographs of him.

By an amazing coincidence, however, a photograph of my grandfather appeared in The Scots Magazine nearly forty years after his death, during October 1984. It accompanied a letter from a reader who had met him on the road, in Scotland, many years earlier and taken his picture.

Life is truly surprising. The way in which my grandfather's story suddenly resurfaced, so many years after his death, is staggering. As a result of that letter, and others which followed, I discovered much more about him. So much more, in fact, that his life has provided the inspiration for a book I intend to write next year. It will have a simple title: The Rovin Boy.

My eldest brother, Jim, had the same sense of adventure as our grandfather. He was a natural risk taker and a natural business-man. As a child, he would leave for school with some cheap toy, and many deals later return home with a radio or record player, often causing my mother apoplexy!

Jim went bankrupt twice in his life. He first went bankrupt at the tender age of 20, on bad legal advice, after a crook of a customer failed to settle an account for some building work. Jim was thrown out of his home, together with his wife and two young children, within six weeks of the bankruptcy. In the years that followed he rebuilt his building business, employing more than 50 men at times. He then repaid all his bankruptcy debts, although he was under no legal obligation to do so.

More than twenty years later, he went bankrupt a second time.

This was in 1978 after he had diversified into farming. This time he was caught out on a tax bill. He fought that second bankruptcy so hard that he had two heart attacks. By then he had five grown-up and two young children, one with a heart defect.

Jim was, however, a gentle giant of a man, a born adventurer, a character larger than life. He, like me, took his Scottish roots seriously. After spending five years dealing with all the problems associated with his heart attacks and his bankruptcy, early in 1983 he left his home town of Lancaster and took himself and his family to Monkstadt Steading, a small piece of land in the far north of the Isle of Skye. The second bankruptcy had broken his spirit. He was never the same man again, although he tried hard to be, and he subsequently died in 1989 after a heart operation failed.

Outraged by my brother's treatment in bankruptcy, I founded the Association of Bankrupts as we were then known, literally as Jim was in the process of moving to Scotland. A link between Scotland and the Association was formed, right from the outset. That link with Scotland has developed over many years, and many other links forged too, Scotland has its own distinct bankruptcy system, different in several ways to that found in the rest of Britain. Bankruptcy in Scotland is often referred to as sequestration. Both terms are used in this chapter. They mean the same thing.

By the time my brother died in 1989, we had developed a strong Scottish section of the Association. Jim Freer, a bankrupt from Ayrshire, ran the Scottish side of our Association on a voluntary basis. We have had several happy meetings with our members in Scotland and, I for one, am always happy north of the border.

It was therefore appropriate that as the slump broke over the shores of Britain in June 1991, I was to be found on the Isle of Arran with Gill and other then officers of the Association at Blackwaterfoot, overlooking the magical Mull of Kintyre. My own financial affairs were in a mess, as were those of the Association. I had been earning a living as a freelance writer since 1986, running the Association voluntarily. My writing commissions had by then dried up due to the slump, and the income of the Association was barely meeting basic expenses. We had 1000 members then, paying annual subscriptions of just five pounds a year.

It was make or break time, for me, and for the Bankruptcy

Association. I had house repossession proceedings coming against me shortly, because I had fallen into arrears with my mortgage. The lack of writing work had virtually eliminated my income. I spent the last £500 I had to my name on the meeting on Arran. Looking back, it was an act of pure madness. I was staring ruin in the face, not for the first time in my life I hasten to add, and probably not for the last time either. I felt, therefore, that there was nothing to lose by calling this meeting.

The meeting was critical. We made some important decisions. We changed the name of the Association to our present name, raised our subscription to £15 a year and, very importantly, we decided I should write an advice book, Bankruptcy – The Reality and the Law, and publish it ourselves. It was all a risk, a big risk, like life itself, but it worked. We sold nearly 10,000 copies of this book in the following two years alone. It was a huge success.

My home was saved, although no thanks to the judge in my county court who did his best to deprive me of it, despite my having a disabled wife. The Association survived too, and the hectic period that followed, I have already described in an earlier chapter.

Nearly a year before our important gathering on the Isle of Arran, we had an important meeting of another sort. On Friday 13 July 1990 I went, with others, to see George Kerr, the Accountant in Bankruptcy for Scotland. This was our first meeting with him, as an Association. It seemed a highly appropriate date for the man in charge of Scottish bankruptcy administration to see us!

Arriving in Edinburgh with Jim Freer and Kay Short, then both officers of the Association, I was immediately attracted to the magnificent architecture of this capital city. Even more striking was the proud, confident bearing of its citizens and their exceptionally gracious manners.

When we arrived at the offices of Mr Kerr at Drumsheugh Gardens, just off Princess Street, our initial good impressions were reinforced with our courteous reception. At two in the afternoon with refreshment of coffee quickly provided, we settled down to our meeting which was to last nearly three and a half hours.

I began by briefly explaining the background to our Association and by pointing out the strong emotional links we had with Scotland. My eldest brother, whose bankruptcy experiences had led to the foundation of our Association, had died in Edinburgh only the previous September. This added a poignant touch to our Association's many other links with Scotland. I felt very much on home ground.

We quickly launched into what was to become a recurring issue throughout the meeting – the explosion of bankruptcies in Scotland since the introduction of the 1985 Bankruptcy (Scotland) Act. More than 500 sequestrations took place in Scotland in May of 1990 alone, a figure which, if it were matched pro rata in England, would be equivalent to 60,000 bankruptcies a year – more than fivefold the then current rate!

We wanted to know what on earth was going on. Scottish newspapers were ablaze with stories of the increase in bankruptcies. Concern was being expressed about the causes and the cost to the taxpayer of administrating the many cases where there were no assets. Mr Kerr had no real answers although he rejected some suggestions made in the press that the increase was because trustees were encouraging unnecessary bankruptcies, in order to increase their fee income.

He did, however, feel the Scottish bankruptcy process was now far too 'user friendly' – a debtor could simply sign away his worries. This was encouraging advice agencies to push debtors down the bankruptcy avenue, without giving proper thought to the very serious implications of bankruptcy, for those involved.

Mr Kerr estimated that around 85 per cent of all Scottish bankruptcies were consumer bankruptcies. He said that true business bankruptcies remained at about the 300 a year mark, which was about the same as pre–1985 levels. He seemed relieved when we explained that our then 550 member strong Association consisted of and represented the entrepreneurial and professional section of the community. They had gone bankrupt because of business failure.

He responded to criticisms I made of the Insolvency Service in England along the lines of: 'This is Scotland, we do things differently here.' He implied they behaved better. He also backed these assertions with the promise that any bankrupt in Scotland could speak to him personally on any bankruptcy issue, and said he would advise them when he could.

Mr Kerr explained about the new system of block fees that was being introduced in Scotland. This new system was intended to cut the heavy costs to the public purse of administrating sequestrations. He also told us that he was working on an official advice leaflet for bankrupts in Scotland, and that he would consult with us about the content of this.

The meeting was conducted throughout in a thoroughly courteous and civilised manner. It ended quite naturally when we felt we had explored all the major avenues of immediate concern to our Association. As the meeting concluded at five thirty, it was agreed that we would meet again as required, and that we should now open up a permanent line of communication by letter and telephone. We shook hands and parted, well satisfied on our part, and impressed by Mr Kerr's firm personal hold over the Scottish bankruptcy scene, a grip that continues to this day.

We made our way to Princess Street, and a magnificent Georgian bar, to enjoy the pleasures of a few pints of 'heavy' and other famous local beverages. We all felt that the discussions had been excellent and that this was one Friday the 13th which would not prove unlucky, and that nothing but good would flow from our meeting that day.

As we entered Edinburgh station next morning to catch our trains home, a lone piper on the castle ramparts high above us struck up a sad, but magnificent lament. I thought of it as a salute to my dead brother, who loved his Scottish roots so much, and to the links our Association had now firmly established with Scotland.

Two years later, on 3 July 1992 I headed north to Dunblane. The next day, American Independence Day, we held a meeting for Scottish members. Member of Parliament, Margaret Ewing, was in attendance with her husband, Fergus Ewing, a Glasgow lawyer. There was a good turn out of about 20 members of our small, but important Scottish branch.

I spoke at length about the affairs of the Association and Margaret Ewing told us of her involvement with the committee dealing with a new Scottish Bankruptcy Bill then going through Parliament. She told us she was going to transmit our concerns to that committee. She kept her promise and her many references to our Association and its concerns are written up in Hansard. Margaret Ewing also expressed admiration for the fact that we could attract more members to our meetings than her own political party, the Scottish Nationalists, could attract to their meetings.

The excellent support for our work from Scotland has been one of the few gems of joy in what has been a long struggle. We have also received help and support from several insolvency practitioners north of the border. In particular, Alan O'Boyle of Walkers in Glasgow has shown terrific interest and offered much practical help and advice. He has proved a real supporter, and a gentleman.

Colin Hastings of Hastings and Company in Glasgow has also proved helpful. I first came across Colin when I had an exchange of views with him on BBC Radio Scotland. This was during an hour long programme on bankruptcy in 1991. Afterwards he was very helpful in providing information for the first guidebook we published. We have given numerous talks at various events in Scotland since 1991. It is as if there is a natural affinity, between Scotland and the Bankruptcy Association.

Our relationship with Scotland, however, has not been entirely all sweetness and light. In June 1993 I went, together with Jim Freer and Fergus Ewing, to see George Kerr, the Accountant in Bankruptcy, again. Changes in Scottish law had again taken place whereby Scotland was now to have its own mini insolvency service. In effect, this was to give George Kerr's department of civil servants charge of the administration of many bankruptcies. Previously, these had all been handled by private insolvency practitioners.

I laid my own personal laws down to him, telling him how I expected him to treat people, along with a few other home truths. He bridled somewhat, and was clearly rattled by the complete grilling that the three of us there gave him. Times had changed, the slump was now in full flood, and we were an angry Association, determined to have our say.

I could tell that George Kerr was shocked by the very different atmosphere to that at our first friendly meeting in 1990. Fergus Ewing raised many tetchy legal points that began to irritate Mr Kerr, and Jim Freer followed through in similar fashion. Finally, I let fly at him, venting the full fury and might of our Association. I told him that this was the last time I would ever meet with him formally, that I could see no purpose to future meetings, that I simply expected him to treat bankrupt people properly or he would hear from me. He was angry and I think he came close to throwing a punch at me. He did, however, manage to contain himself.

Since our first meeting two years earlier many things had been changed on the Scottish scene, too complex to outline here. I certainly had no kind thoughts about Scottish bankruptcy law. New legislation had been rushed through Parliament bringing in a new bankruptcy system which made it difficult for Scottish debtors to bankrupt themselves. Fergus Ewing had made a personal trip to Parliament and had met the Scottish Minister responsible for overseeing the Bill. The conversation that took place between them was ludicrous, and not printable here. Fergus Ewing's report to me on these matters had made me very angry and Mr Kerr had cause to be on a short fuse too. He was then only employed on an annual, renewable contract. The upset at this meeting was, therefore, not altogether unexpected.

As we left Mr Kerr's office, the atmosphere was terse and our good wishes and farewells to each other were a little frozen. The Bankruptcy Association had, yet again, presented a strong case.

9

Ireland

The Bankruptcy Association, since it was formed in 1983, has also been heavily involved with both Southern and Northern Ireland. One of the first people to join was Terry Crosbie, an accountant from Waterford in Southern Ireland. He is not, and never has been bankrupt, but has continued to support the Association for more than a decade.

The laws in Northern Ireland are now in line with those to be found in England, Wales and Scotland, less primitive than those in the South of Ireland. The bankruptcy laws in Southern Ireland are based on the much harsher English laws which prevailed at the turn of the century. People are held in bankruptcy for much longer periods than elsewhere and I have often wondered if Irish legislators are aware that this is the twentieth century.

Impassioned speeches made by two Bankruptcy Association members from Southern Ireland who attended one of our national meetings paid testimony to the horrendous social consequences of being made bankrupt in Southern Ireland. Even today, it is not unusual for Irish bankrupts to be ostracised by their local communities, particularly if they live in a small town or village.

I have strong family connections with Ireland, too. My maternal grandfather was an Irishman. He was in the Irish Guards and

61

fought in the battle of the Somme, as did my paternal grandfather. My grandfathers were both wounded in that battle.

My eldest son, John did a tour of duty with the army, helping to police Northern Ireland, just before his deployment to the Gulf. As I write, in August 1994, there is strong talk at last of an expected cessation of hostilities by the IRA, after their 25 year campaign of terror.

William, my youngest brother, fell in love with Ireland and an Irish girl, Stephanie, whom he married. Some of my fondest memories are of visits to the beautiful Wicklow mountains, south of Dublin, where William and Stephanie set up home.

The tragic and premature death of William has not marred these fond memories. The personal links with Ireland live on, through William's wife and children, and through the many members of the Bankruptcy Association which we have on each side of the border.

One of my happiest memories is of sailing, in mountainous seas, from Holyhead in Wales to Dun Laoghaire in Ireland to attend William's wedding. It was September 1983, and although I was then 36 years old, it was like going back to childhood. My parents and most of my eleven brothers and sisters were on the ship with me. My poor mother, who was no sailor, was very ill below deck with my father, while the rest of us gathered together on a higher deck, just beneath the ship's bridge.

We stood, arms around each other, mesmerised by the huge waves crashing over the bow of the ship. If the ship had foundered that September evening, in those stormy seas, we would not have cared. We were children again, brothers and sisters together.

Ireland, and a wonderful wedding lay ahead. For a few days, that beautiful land was to set us free from our adult worries and responsibilities. As the ship ploughed into huge wave after huge wave, we were enthralled by the mighty power of the sea and gripped by a feeling of pure exhilaration.

10

Battlefield Honours

This book has largely concentrated on the activities of myself and Gill Hankey. It was Gill who came to the rescue of the Bankruptcy Association after our magical meeting on the Isle of Arran in 1991. It was Gill who saw I was on my knees with the pressure then upon me. She quietly picked up the single rifle and few rounds of ammunition that was my sole weapon, propped me against a wall for a rest, took aim at the huge problems in the country that were steadily overwhelming me, and calmly fired, hitting a target every time.

It is entirely appropriate therefore, that the opening chapter of this book starts with her name. I wish, however to pay tribute here to the many other people, aside from Gill, who have made huge contributions to this story.

I founded the Bankruptcy Association early in 1983, literally as my eldest brother Jim left our home town of Lancaster for the Isle of Skye, shattered by the events surrounding his second bankruptcy. It was a special moment. My wife Jean, my brother Jim, another brother David, and a good friend of mine, Francis Allison, sat around the dining table in my home whilst I outlined my plans to do something about our bankruptcy laws. The minutes of that meeting are still preserved. David had his doubts about calling ourselves the Association for Bankrupts, our planned name, feeling this might be off putting. A printing error subsequently turned us into the Association of Bankrupts, an even sharper title.

A few days after that meeting, I wrote a letter to every national newspaper in Britain, announcing the formation of the Association. Only one published it – The Times, that most famous and first national newspaper of Great Britain. My letter appeared in it on Saturday 5 March 1983, as the last tiny entry on a page of readers' letters.

I only heard about its publication the following Monday, from another brother, Andrew. He arrived at my home telling me his solicitor had read my letter in The Times. They both seemed impressed and I was thrilled beyond imagination. I never actually saw that published letter until Gill tracked it down for me, nearly a decade later, during 1992. It is now framed and hangs on my office wall.

I was a schoolteacher at the time at a local school. I expected a flood of mail, something that neither materialised then, nor has done since. Little did I realise, but a long struggle was only just beginning.

I received just one letter in response to my letter in The Times. It was from Stephen Aris, then a reporter with The Sunday Times, who had just begun researching a book on bankruptcy. This was later published under the title 'Going Bust.' He came to see me and my brother Jim, who was then travelling backwards and forwards between Lancaster and Skye. The amazing story of the Bankruptcy Association began to unfold.

Shortly after visiting me, Stephen Aris wrote a short piece about the Association in the Sunday Times, and one Roy Whitman, an accountant from Borden in Hampshire wrote to me asking if he could help. Roy Whitman was the first of many amazing people who crept into my life, one by one, some staying for a long time, some just making a brief appearance. They brought to the Bankruptcy Association the magic which has fuelled it, since its inception. I have lived through a very difficult, but also very wonderful time, with these people.

Shortly after Roy Whitman came to my support, Michael Sheldon-Allen, then a bankrupt solicitor living in a bed sit in Cornwall, wrote to me offering his help. Eventually Michael was to write a textbook on bankruptcy with me. This was published by Tolley

Publishing in 1989, the year my brother Jim died. Michael did most of the writing and this textbook was described by the legal editor at Tolley's as: 'The finest legal book I have ever had the privilege to edit.'

On publication, it was heavily criticised by Steve Hill, now a spokesman for the largest firm of insolvency practitioners, Cork Gully. Not withstanding this heavyweight attack, we sold out the first edition of one thousand copies. The publishers then refused to reprint the book. It was disgraceful. Not only could we have sold thousands of copies throughout the slump, but it should never have been withdrawn from sale being an excellent and much needed bankruptcy textbook. I have since often suspected that this action by my publisher formed part of the political attack being applied against me.

These two wonderful characters, Roy Whitman and Michael Sheldon-Allen, supported me through those early years from 1983 to 1990. They are both knights of the Bankruptcy Association. Together, we were the three musketeers, and I salute these two men here.

During 1989 the first lady helper arrived on the scene. Kay Short, then the wife of a bankrupt, offered to help us. She bravely drew down huge press publicity on herself and her family, to draw attention to the existence of our Association. This was a tremendous personal sacrifice, not matched until later, when others arrived on the scene. She was the first member of the Bankruptcy Association prepared to do this in a major way. She also did it at a time when bankrupts were thin on the ground and universally, wrongly, regarded as rogues. If I had one medal only to offer for bravery then I would, without doubt, hand it to Kay Short.

A year after Kay joined our cause, Jim Feer, then a bankrupt in Ayrshire, volunteered to look after the bankrupt community in Scotland. He brought his dry Scottish humour and famous Scottish courage to the Association. He appeared on television and radio programmes throughout Scotland. He pressed our cause hard and through his personal care for members in Scotland he strengthened our hand there enormously.

Kay and Jim are therefore also key players from the past and they must be acknowledged here. I owe both a great debt of gratitude. Whilst the story in this book focuses on Gill and I, it should be made clear that a large number of other people have, over the years, been on stage with us.

Terry Protheroe, from Maidstone, a divorced mother of two young sons, joined us for a time after she was bankrupted. She followed Kay's lead in bravely telling her own story and publicising the Association, at one time, to her great delight, appearing on the Derek Jameson show on BBC Radio 2. Karen Milburn from Belfast did the same in Northern Ireland. For a short time, Margaret Beaman, a bankrupt lady from Sussex manned a special telephone inquiry line in the South of England.

These people, and many others not mentioned here, have been part of the story told in this book. I cannot unfold the whole story, it is too complex and incredible. At the beginning of my book, Bankruptcy – The Reality and the Law, published early in 1992, I described my brother Jim's journey to Skye. In it I told the story of the bend at Uig, a notorious U bend on the Isle of Skye which my brother miraculously circumvented with his mobile home, as he escaped to Skye. The first call I received after publishing that book came from a lady reader.

She told me: 'I have been round that bend at Uig. But mine was in Austria.'

Life is one difficult U bend. I have been round it and back again with the Bankruptcy Association, thanks to all the wonderful people who have helped.

A large part of the cast described in this chapter were at a national meeting of members we held in September 1991 at Liverpool Polytechnic, a few months after we were together on Arran. Roy Whitman was present. Sadly, Michael Sheldon-Allen was absent, he was soon to die of cancer – I miss him to this day.

Jim Freer, Kay Short and Gill Hankey were also there. In addition, Lord Sudeley, then a patron of the Association, was also with us. Lord Sudeley's grandfather had been bankrupted at the turn of the century and the present Lord thought this had been done unfairly and was seeking retrospective justice for his ancestor.

At the end of that meeting Albert Lowe, whose wife Tracey had attended the meeting with the Minister, John Redwood, rose to his feet. Albert, a warm hearted Irishman, with no fine airs or graces, spoke out: 'This Association,' he said, 'must never be allowed to die. It is a beautiful butterfly.' It was a dramatic note on which to end the meeting. I thought then that a butterfly only has a short life. This particular butterfly, however, was to live on, winging its way through the horrors that lay ahead.

PART THREE
The Way Forward

11

The Way Forward

Bankruptcy has some uses. The American railroad system was only built at reasonable cost to its users because hundreds of millions of dollars were lost by investors as they poured money into one bankrupt railroad company after another. Each existing piece of track was, in rapid turn, bought at a knock-down price by successive new railroad companies trying to make them viable. The same was true in Britain and Europe.

From the point of view of commuters, not investors, it would be useful if Eurotunnel, the owners of the channel tunnel, went bust. Any new company taking over would then not be saddled with the huge debts of the old company, and could thus make much lower charges for those using it. Seen in this way, bankruptcy can bring about, in brutal and swift ways, substantial redistributions of economic wealth. Sometimes this is useful to society as a whole, if not to the advantage of a few losers.

The capitalist system is a vast gambling machine with winners and losers, like any other system of gambling. With the collapse of the communist system in the East, it is a system that now seems poised to conquer the world. Even China is developing its own bankruptcy system.

Bankruptcy is a useful, indeed an essential tool, for a capitalist economy. It is a system that calls time on the capitalist gamblers.

It removes the losers from the gambling table when they are threatening to upset the whole system by owing money they cannot repay. It is a neat, simple, efficient and effective way to end the game. However, it can also be brutal, indiscriminate, and unfair.

As we move rapidly towards the twenty first century, we live in a profoundly changed, and rapidly changing, world. We are evolving an increasingly interlinked global economy. There is talk, if not of a world currency, at least of world companies, who put their own economic interests before that of any given country. This is the future. This is where we are inevitably heading, with the exception of a few insignificant countries with sealed borders and economies.

Meantime however, back on the ranch, here in bankrupt Britain, our country faces potential long term economic decline because we cannot get the measure of this new world. Vast technological changes over the past decade mean that goods can be produced with a fraction of the labour force previously needed, leading to mass unemployment. This brings with it an increase in crime and social decay, as well as a real potential for serious social unrest.

The same is true in much of Europe and the rest of the world. These are vast issues, and they will only be solved by determined effort from the business communities and their governments.

I want to pick out just one issue from this vast array of problems and suggest a way forward for us in Britain. It has been widely debated and argued in the eminent journals of The Royal Society for the encouragement of Arts, Manufactures and Commerce that there is a great need to stimulate the growth of small and medium sized companies. This would provide the employment no longer being offered by the giant PLC companies. It is the large companies that have shed the jobs. Shell UK, for example, employed some 20,000 people in 1980. Today, it employs just 10,000 people, yet the scope of its operations is far greater. There are many similar examples.

The only hope for a successful future, for Britain as a nation, is the development of a powerful entrepreneurial culture. The driving force is going to be the hundreds of thousands of graduates now pouring out of business schools and universities each year. These people will have to build their own futures and the future of our country. They will need help, a lot of it. The help needs to be real, not imaginary or illusory.

It should be clear to the reader, from the experiences from the coal face of business described in this book, that it is hard to succeed in business, very hard, but very easy to fail. This is because budding entrepreneurs in Britain are faced with one thousand and one potential ambushes which can bring them quickly to their knees.

In practical terms, it is not really a fair gamble to start a business in modern Britain. It does, in fact, amount to virtual financial suicide on the part of those who try. The reason it is so difficult is, in my firm view, because of a wrong bias in many of our commercial laws.

We live in a complex capitalist society which produces more and more law, literally day by day. Many of our laws are poorly debated and badly put together, and there is much secondary legislation which fills out the bones of primary Acts of Parliament. These pass through a special committee in Parliament, into statute, with scarcely any examination. It is all very shambolic as, indeed, is the Parliamentary process itself.

Throw into this lethal cocktail centuries of grip on primary legislation by the great landowners who ruled England in the past, and the powerful vested commercial interests that so dominate the modern Conservative Party, and you have the perfect mixture to produce what I call 'one sided law.'

Thus the law tends to favour those who have wealth and power against those who do not have it, especially in relation to our commercial laws. For example, leases of all kinds, whether on property or other goods, heavily favour the landlord or owner against the tenant or borrower. Creditors are given extensive rights to pursue debtors, whilst debtors have few sources of protection. Publishing contracts favour the publishers rather than the authors. Employment contracts favour the employer rather than the employed. Building contracts favour main contractors against smaller sub-contractors. Banking documents favour the banks rather than their customers. On and on this list could go, Lloyd's of London, for instance, are virtually unsueable, by virtue of a special Act of Parliament. Not only does the law tend to favour the most powerful of two contracted parties, if it comes to an argument, this group is better placed to afford lawyers to enforce those rights.

This double edged sword of advantage by the powerful commercial interests in the country is wielded with devastating effect against smaller businesses, with whom they deal. It is a long recorded scandal that many large building companies deliberately draw up contracts with their sub-contractors which they know, in advance, will end up in litigation, leading to the bankruptcy of the sub-contractors. Landlords demand 'as normal practice' that someone wanting a lease signs up for 20 years, with upward only rent reviews, and often many other clauses.

The effect of this formidable array of weaponry, employed by the powerful groups in our society against smaller businesses is devastating. Make one mistake, sign the wrong document, and a businessman or woman can be ruined. Thousands of businesses have gone bankrupt during this slump simply because they have been incapable of escaping from the terms of onerous property leases. Others have gone bankrupt through onerous terms for hiring vehicles and/or equipment.

Add to this weaponry the ease with which people and companies can be bankrupted and liquidated, and you have the perfect machine for bigger businesses to wreak havoc amongst smaller businesses. That is precisely what has happened during this slump. Banks have withdrawn overdrafts, quite legally. Landlords have bankrupted thousands of tenants. Big businesses have bankrupted thousands of smaller ones and so on. Our new entrepreneurs, however talented, simply cannot survive this system.

We need wholesale reform of our commercial and bankruptcy laws. We need fewer laws, more carefully thought out, allowing for simpler, clearer and fairer contractual arrangements between trading partners and others. The only people who can really understand the state of our country's commercial laws are those who have experienced them at first hand. They need to be seen and experienced to be believed. Those who have suffered by the system are appalled by it.

Society, by its nature, and the nature of life, will have its winners and losers. Surely, however, we can create a better Britain than we currently inhabit. At least let us establish a fair set of ground rules which will help the young, intelligent entrepreneurs who will have the responsibility for building a better tomorrow. The commercial world, as it stands, is a cesspool where newcomers are drowned before they can even learn to swim, by sharks who inhabit its depths.

It is time for change. For real change.

12

Towards the Second Millennium

The final chapter of this book is being written early on the morning of 26 August 1994, just before the last bank holiday of the year. I said in the foreword that the words simply poured onto the pages. They did. Since then, however, Gill Hankey and I have spent many, many hours editing the book, polishing it up to what we hope is a high standard. Almost exactly two months after Gill and I caught our trains to London, it is now reaching completion today.

We held a meeting of the Bankruptcy Association in the George Hotel, Huddersfield on Saturday 20 August 1994. Nearly 30 members of our Association, mainly from Yorkshire, were in attendance that fine Saturday evening. As our battered and bruised members arrived one by one at the hotel, Gill and I greeted them, chatting to each one in turn.

The first couple to arrive were long-standing members Cliff and Ruby Williams. They are not, and never have been bankrupt, but having run their own business for more than 30 years they understand how difficult it is to survive, and have suffered many near misses.

Then Ann Leigh arrived. She was one of the first people to join the Bankruptcy Association more than a decade ago, and was also one of the first members I met personally in those early days. A schoolteacher for many years, Ann had formed a company providing coach tours to France, and had gone bankrupt as a result. She picked up the pieces, however, and has continued running the same business ever since.

Now more than ten years later, she had arrived at our meeting in Huddersfield, her home town. It was a special, moving moment when we met up again and we gave each other a big hug.

I had decided earlier to read part of chapter two of this book at the meeting. As Anne and the other members gathered around Gill and I, it seemed highly appropriate. After reading for twenty minutes or so, I turned to Gill, who was by my side, and asked: 'Was that OK?'

Gill gave me a strange look. Her mind was focused on our members and their reaction to my talk. 'It was fine, John,' she said.

I turned back to face our audience and gradually became aware of the stunned silence that Gill had obviously noticed. This silence must have lasted at least ten seconds. Suddenly, there was a burst of loud, simultaneous applause. I knew then, as members clapped their approval, that this book does indeed speak for the entire bankrupt community of Britain. I was moved beyond any words I can write in this book. It was a moment of pure magic.

It is a great pity that our politicians do not realise the magic that lies within the British people. I doubt if any of our current political leaders would recognise a vision of the future, even if they bumped into one on the road to Damascus. Our political parties are still dinosaurs of the past.

The Bankruptcy Association will move determinedly forwards towards the next century, pressing our call for a fair and sensible society. It will no doubt be as much of a struggle for us in the future as it has been in the past. We will, however, be in there fighting for our children's tomorrow.

Anyone reading this book, suffering from some present or future injustice, will find Gill and I, God willing, battling on. We can both be found at The Bankruptcy Association, 4 Johnson Close, Abraham Heights, Lancaster, LA1 5EU. Tel: 0524 64305.

Epilogue

Life is certainly stranger than fiction. I have lived through amazing times, experienced many adventures and achieved the near impossible. Of one thing I am certain. There is a power outside of me that drives the Bankruptcy Association. This book, like everything else connected to the Bankruptcy Association, has been touched by that power.

Incredible, sometimes unbelievable, coincidences have marked each step of the path I have followed for more than ten years. Two long-standing members of the Association, whom I had not seen for many years, appear in the opening chapter. Similarly, three long-standing members appear in the last chapter.

In addition, several members of the Bankruptcy Association are currently holidaying on the Isle of Skye for the first time. They are staying in cottages which my nephew, my brother Jim's son, has just renovated, fulfilling his father's dream. It was my brother Jim who inspired me to found the Bankruptcy Association during his retreat to Skye, after his second bankruptcy.

Furthermore – a million to one chance this – we are currently in the middle of a battle to save the home of Roddy McDougall. He is a bankrupt who actually resides on the Isle of Skye with his wife Ruth and their children.

Islands and water appear everywhere in the story of the Bankruptcy Association. The drama of the sea, whether angry or calm, seems to mirror the changing feelings which Gill and I experience each day running the Association. The Association is itself an island, a safe haven offering the hope of rescue for those floundering in stormy waters.

The story told in this book will inspire some people, evoke jealousy in others, generate anger and fury in some twisted minds and, if the events of the last 10 years are anything to judge by, will be met with indifference by those who have the power to improve our country.

Bankrupt people, like no other comparable group in Britain, are universally abandoned to their fate. They are sometimes even deserted by those close to them. This incredible story has unfolded because I, for one, was not prepared to abandon a brother I loved.

John McQueen
Lancaster
Saturday 27 August 1994

If you lived in the richest, most powerful city it was possible for a man to imagine, but there was no love there, no mercy and no justice for those who met with misfortune; then you would be better off dead than to live in such a place.